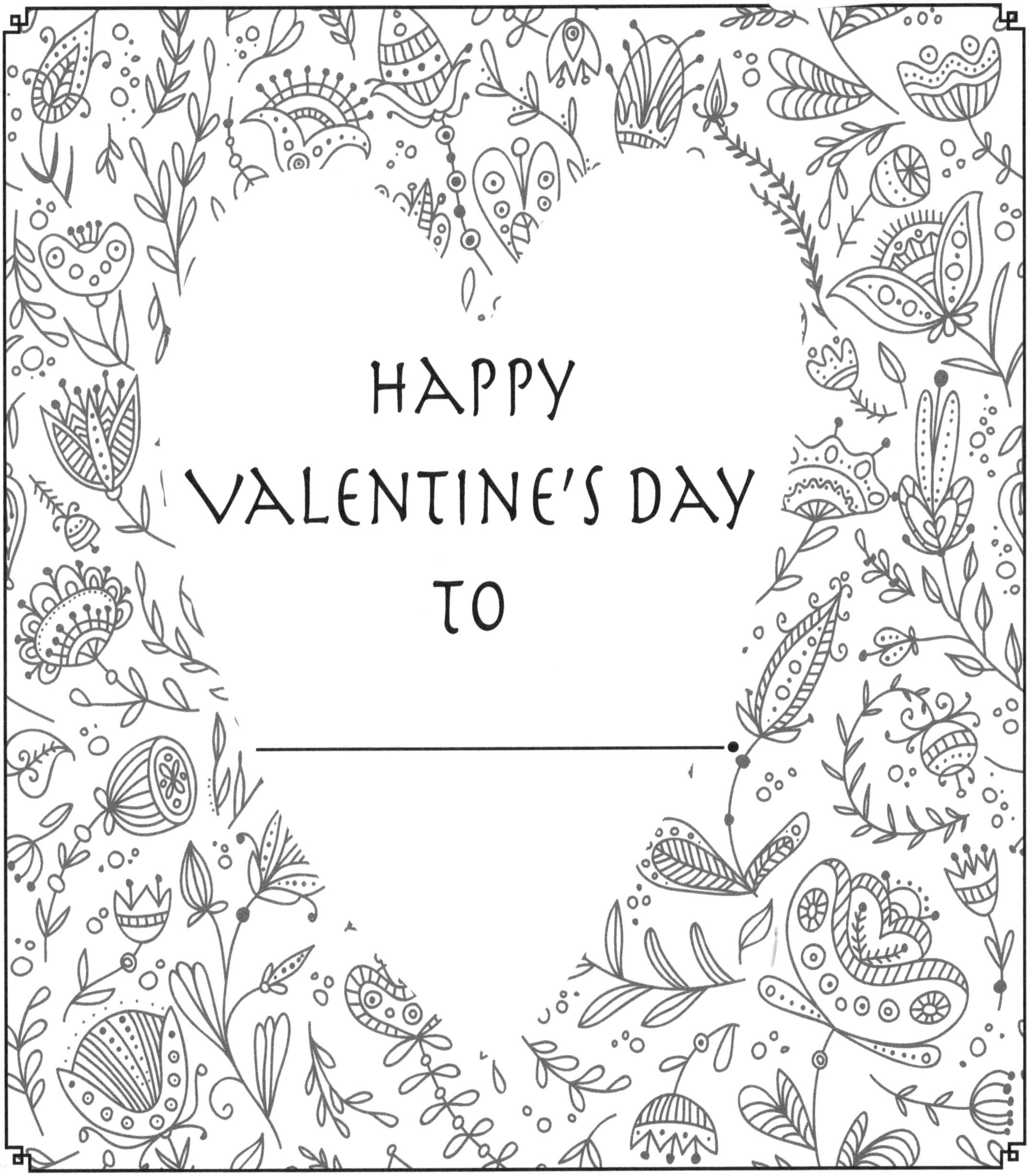
HAPPY
VALENTINE'S DAY
TO

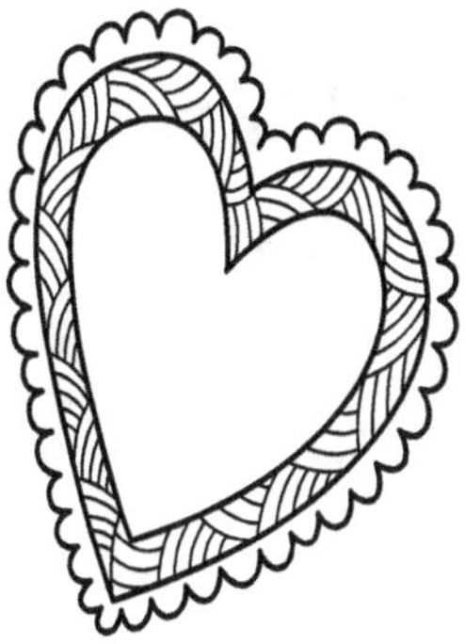

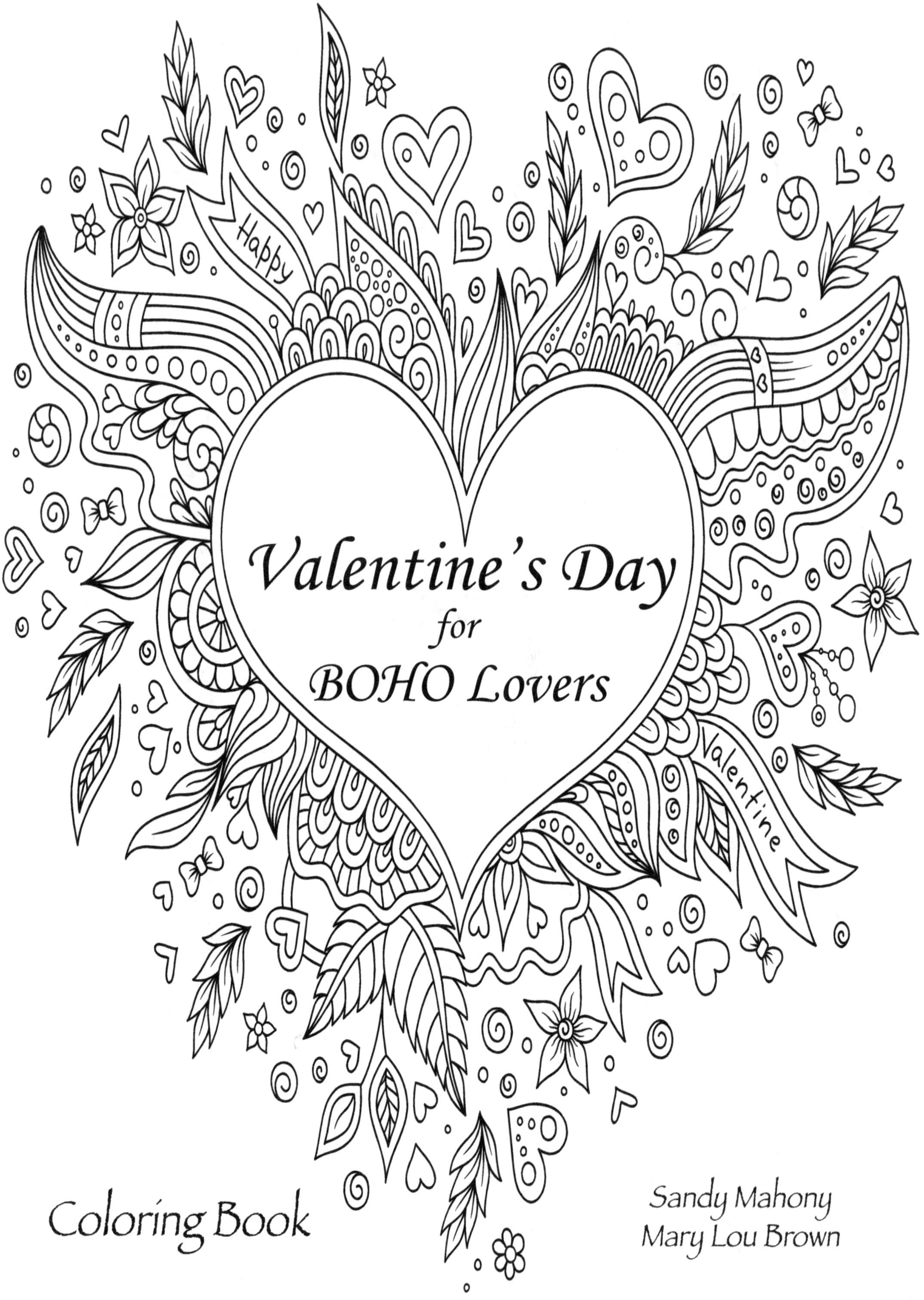

Coloring Book

Sandy Mahony
Mary Lou Brown

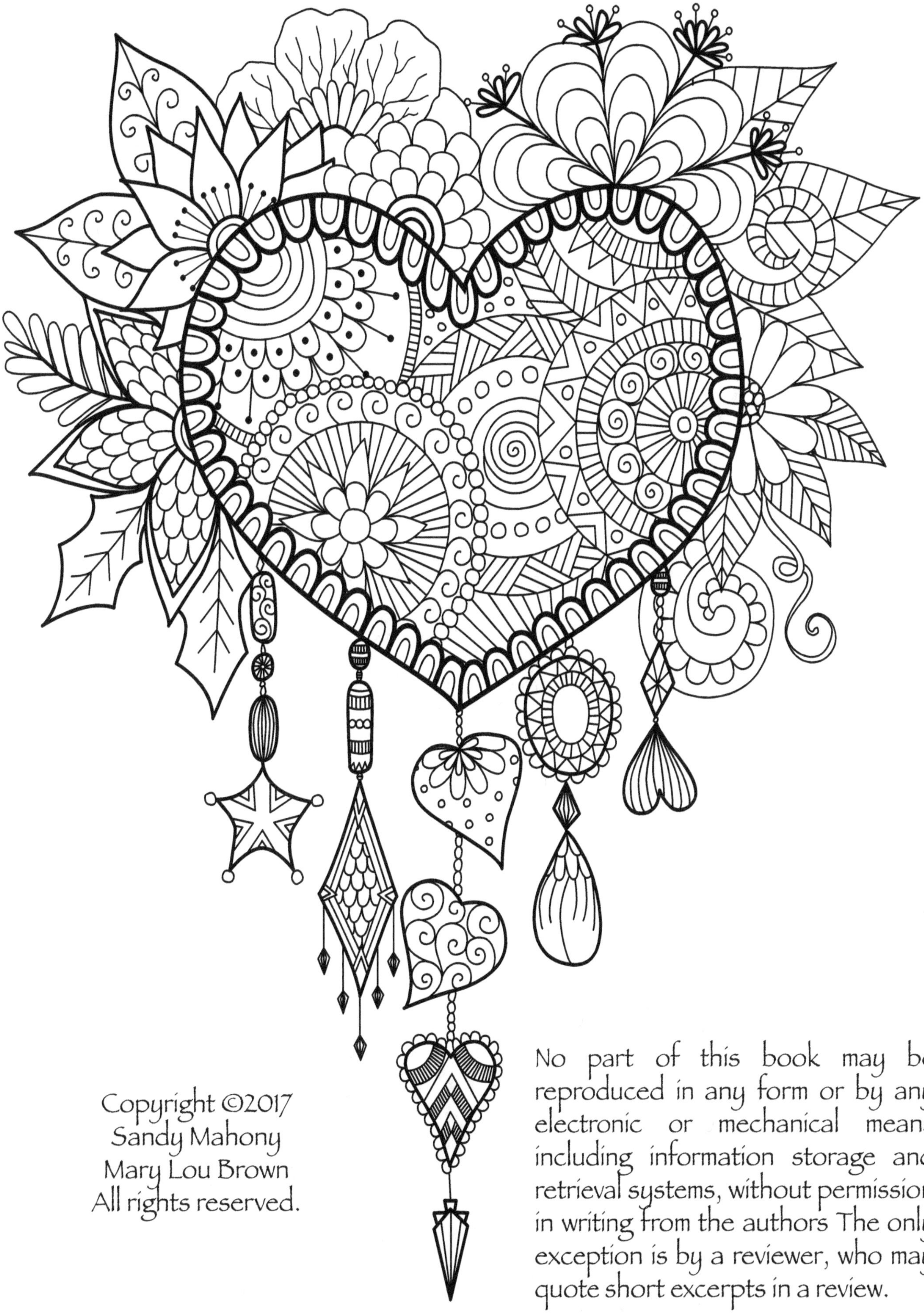

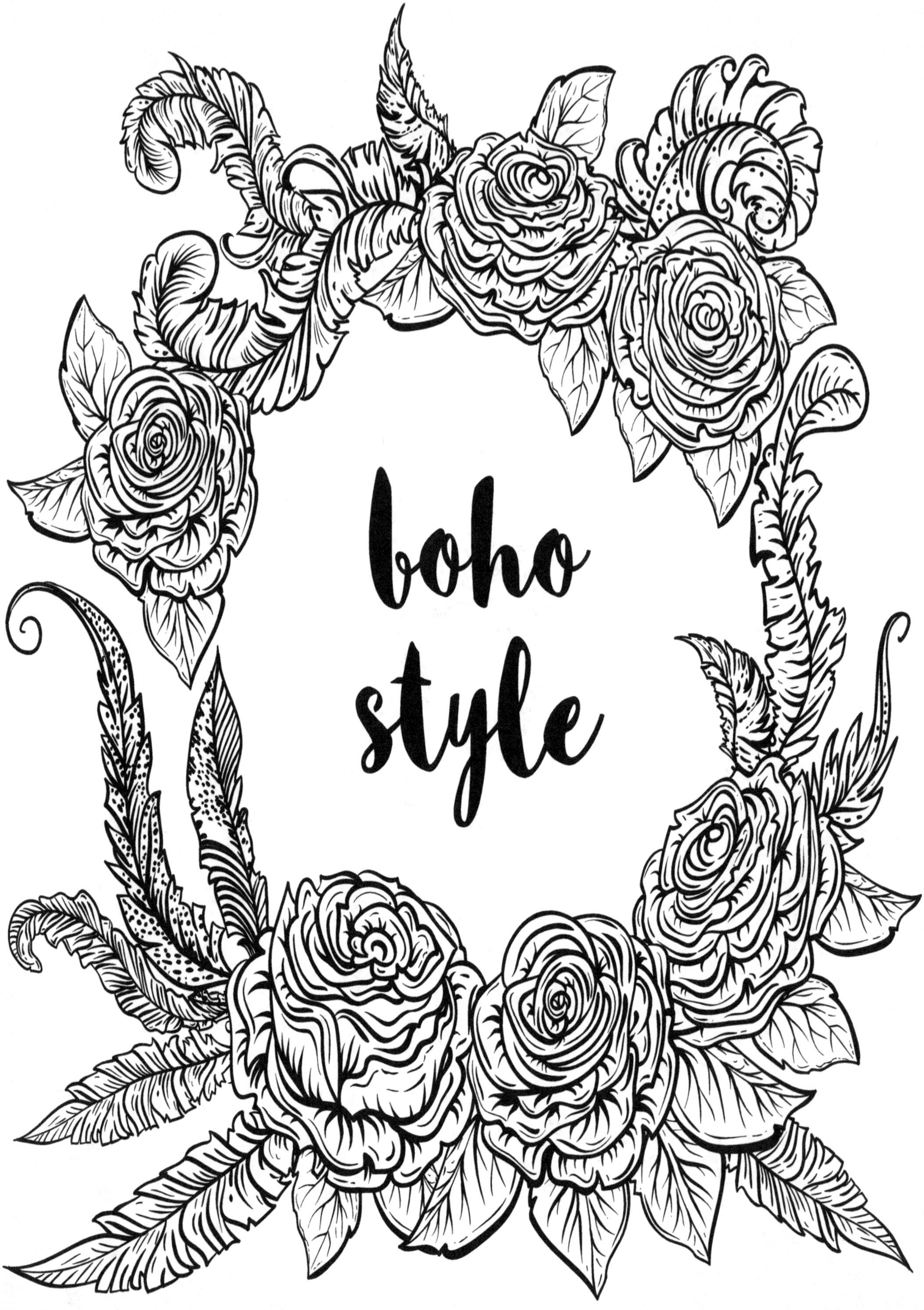
boho
style

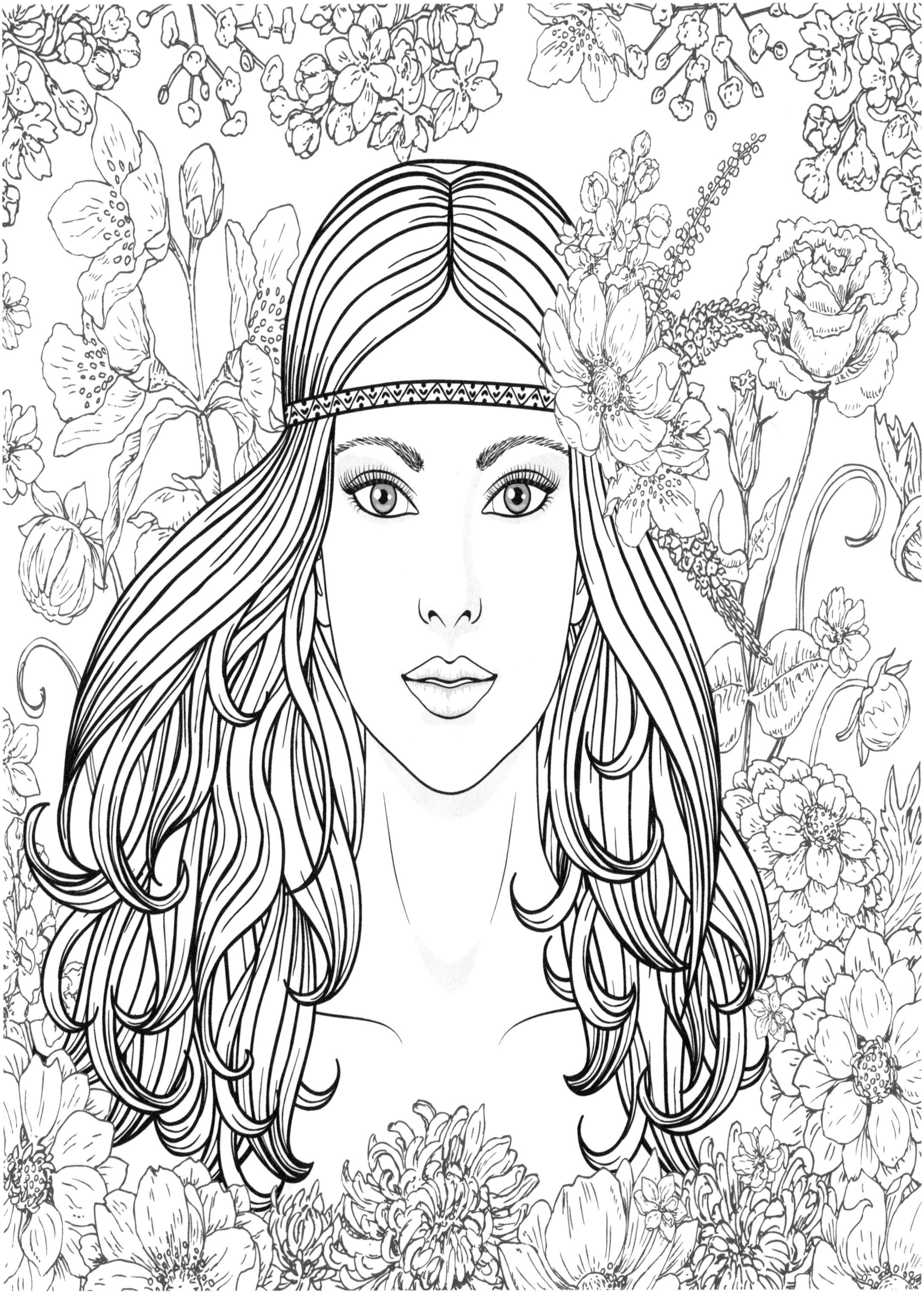

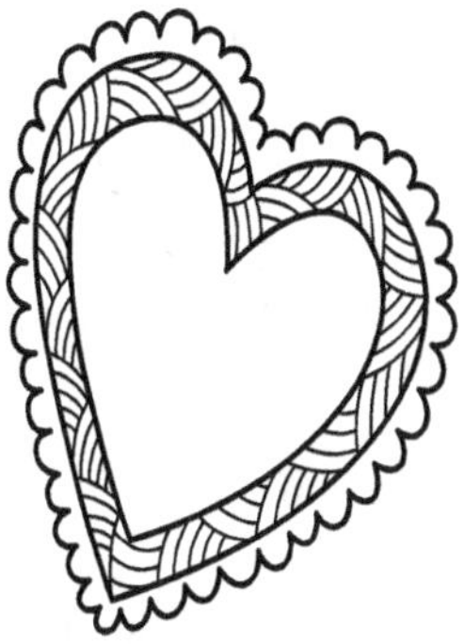

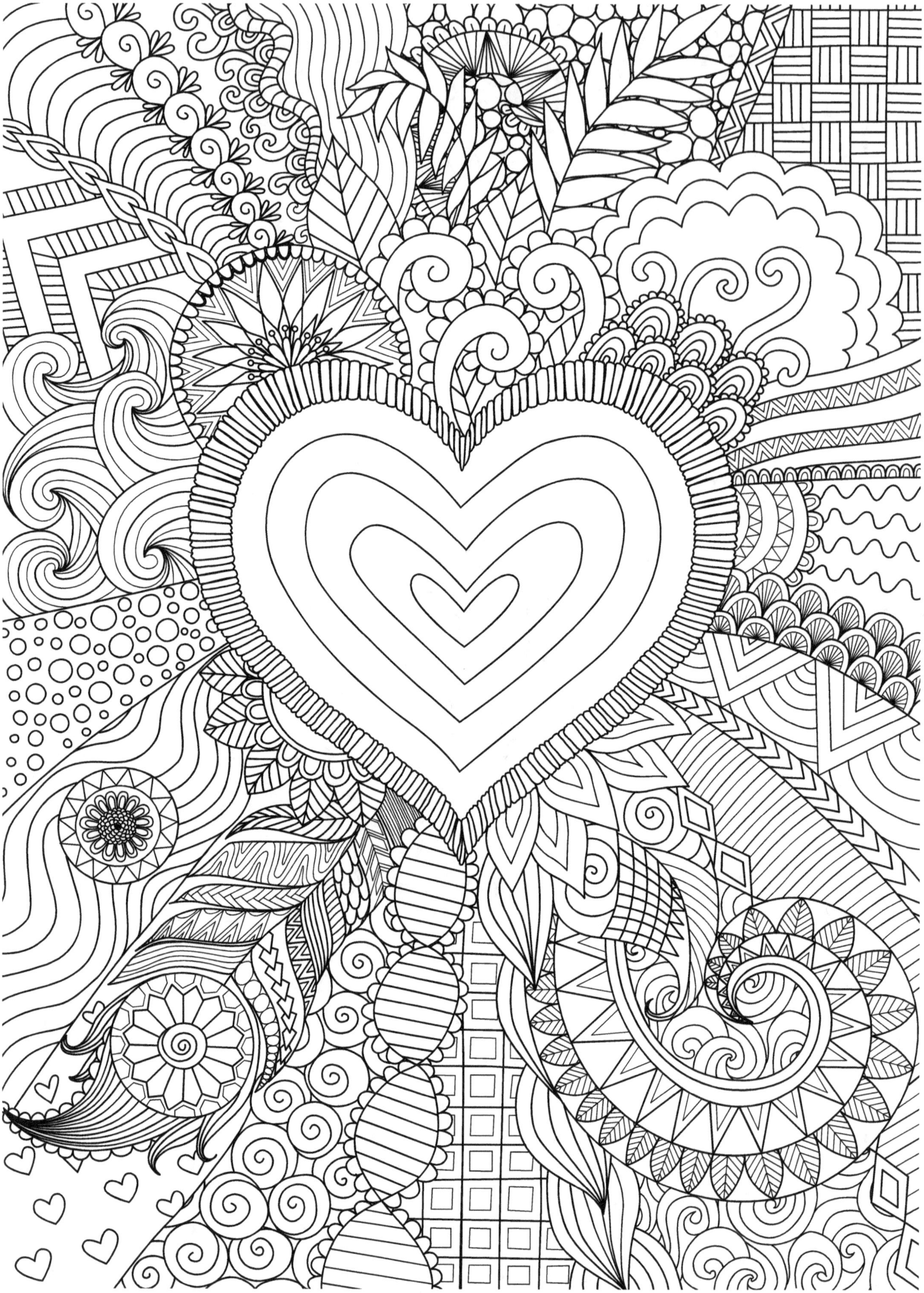

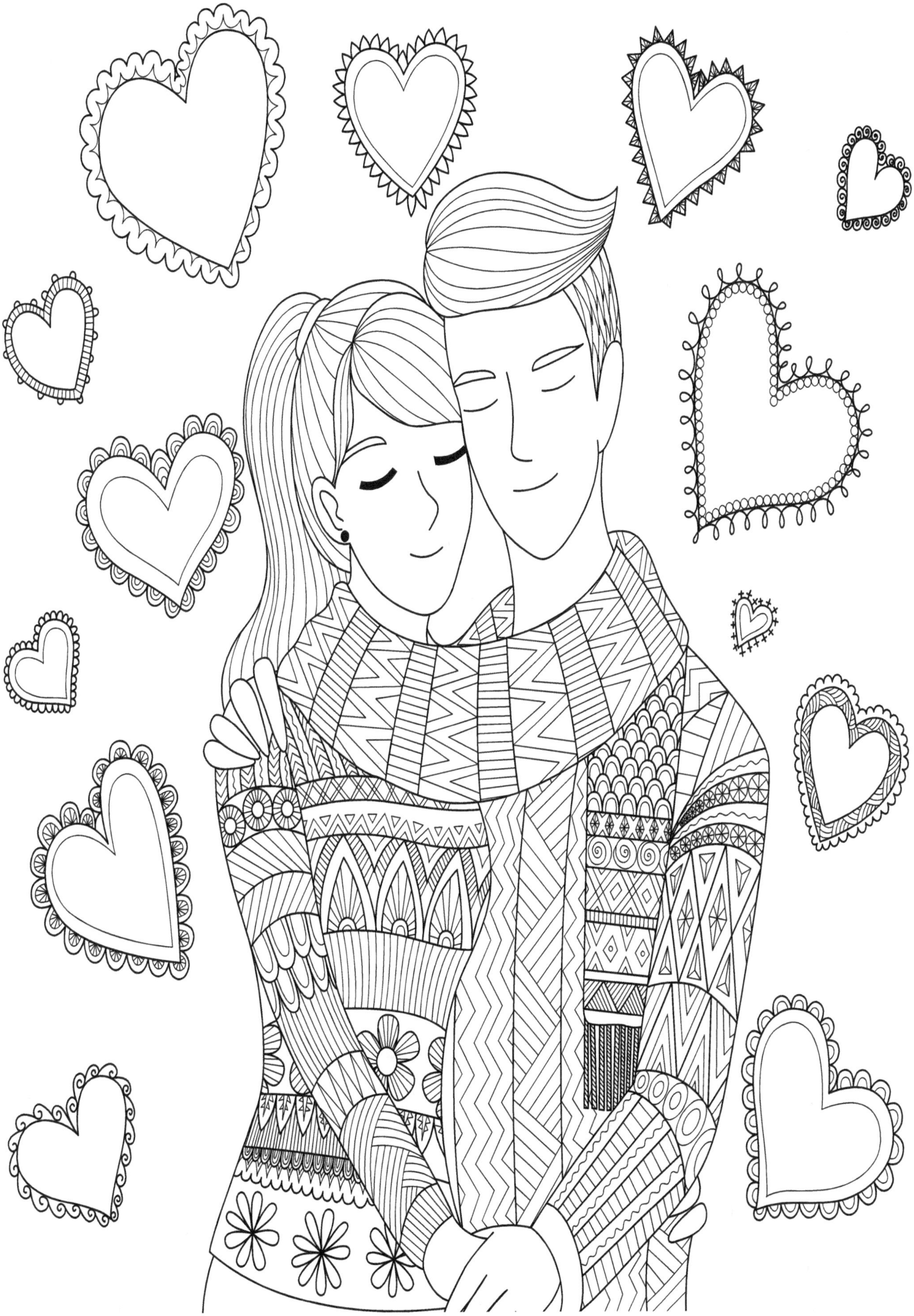

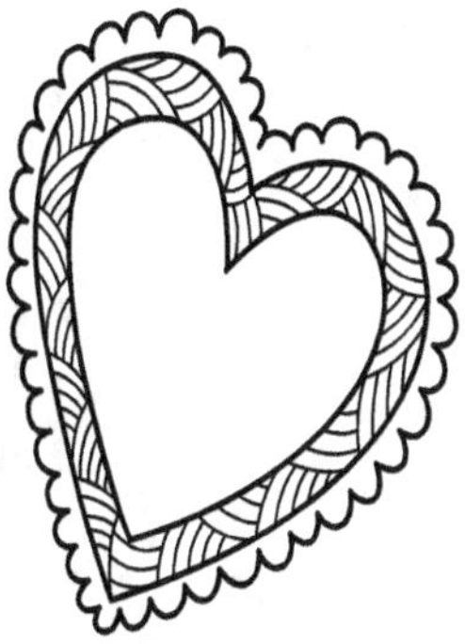

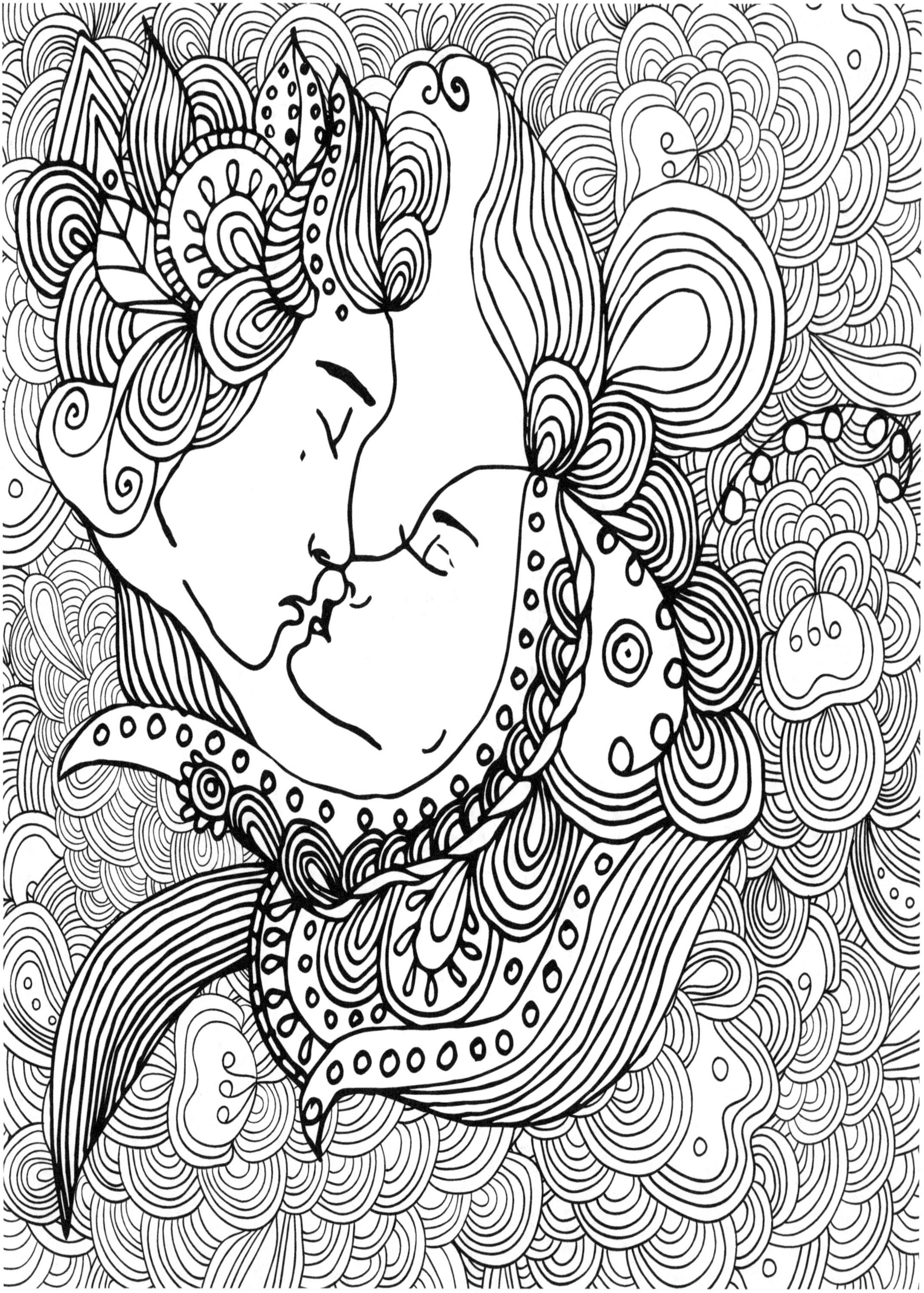

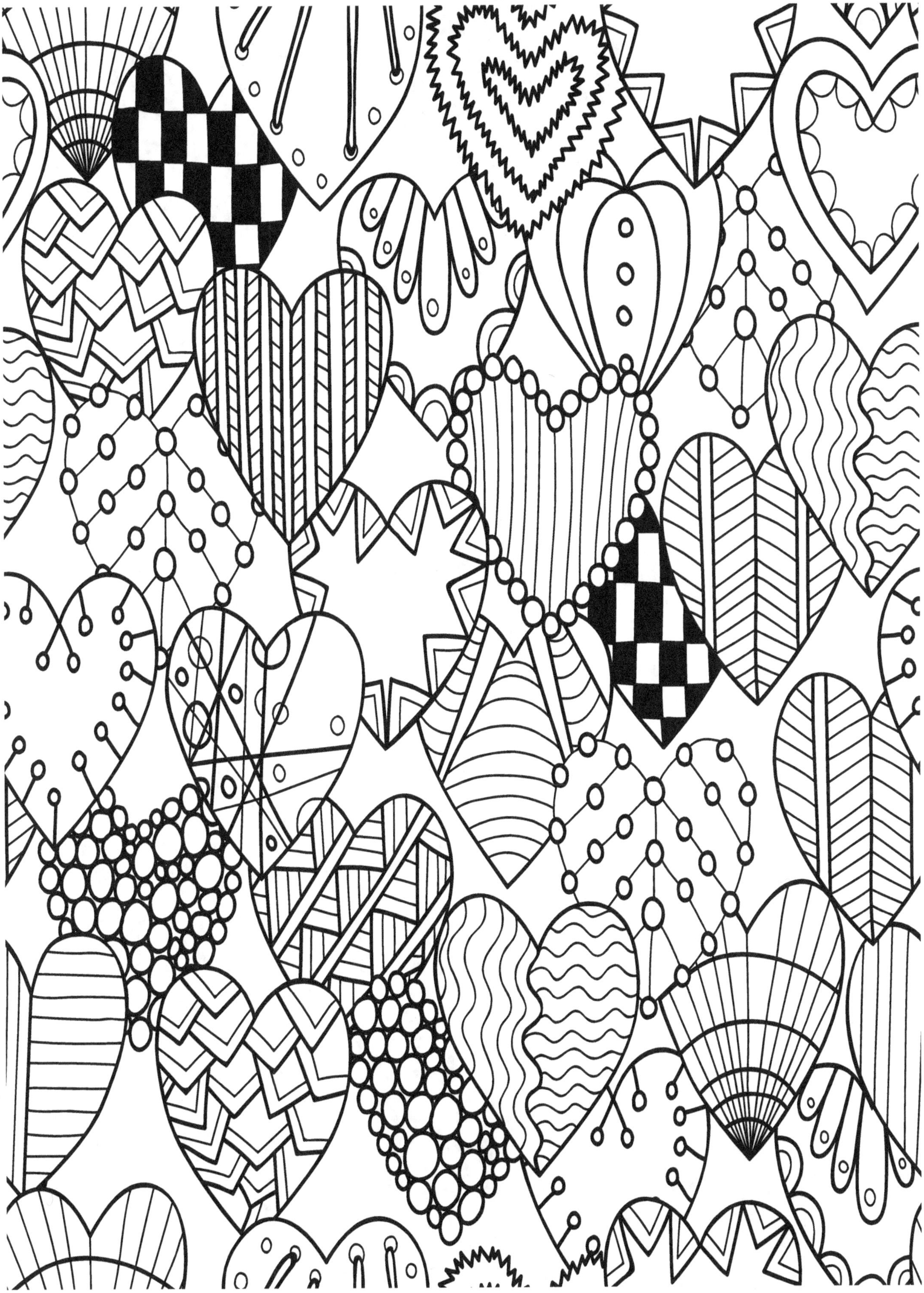

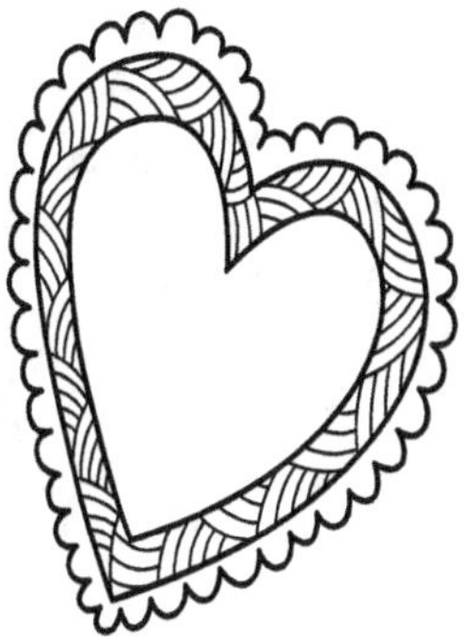

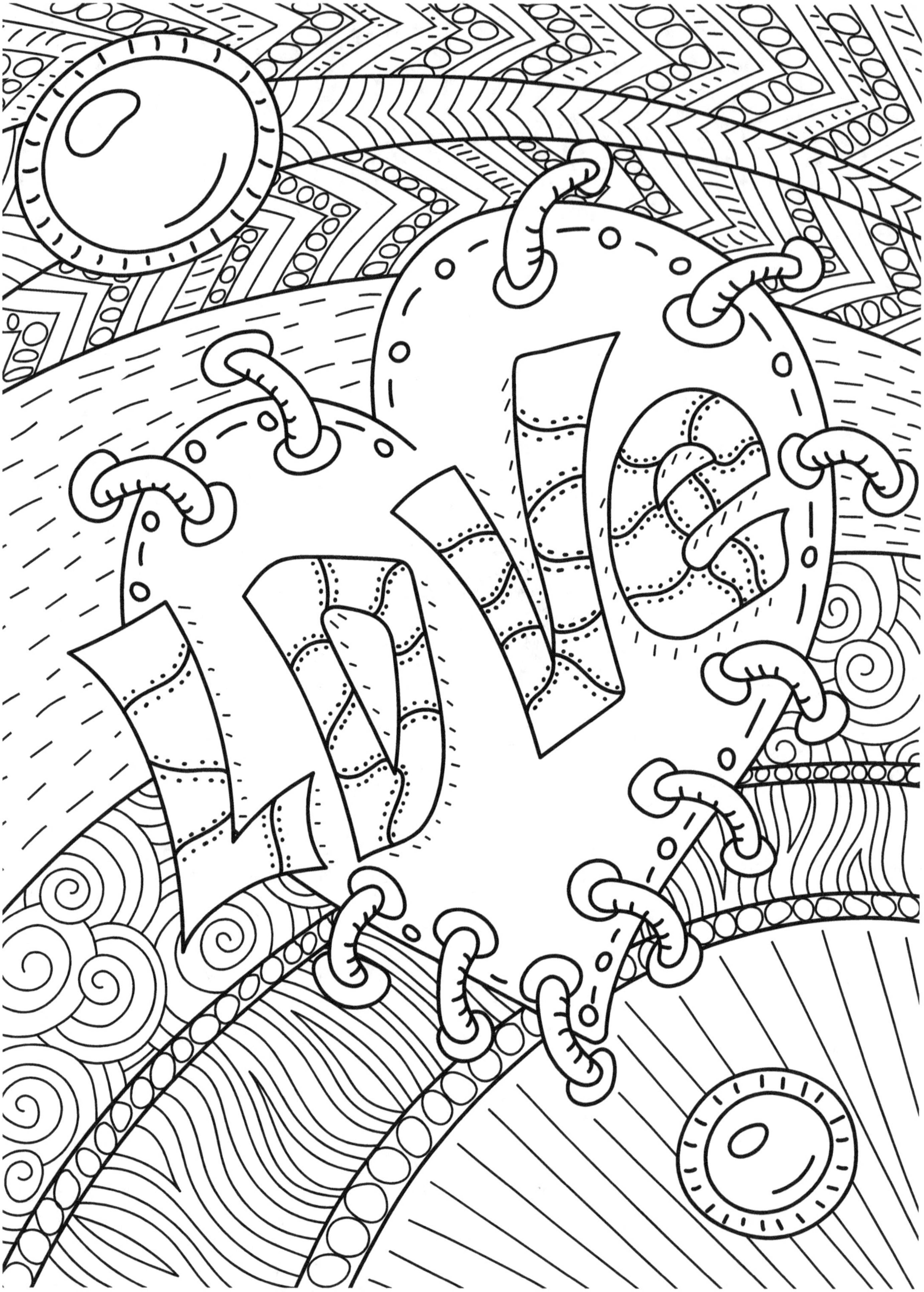

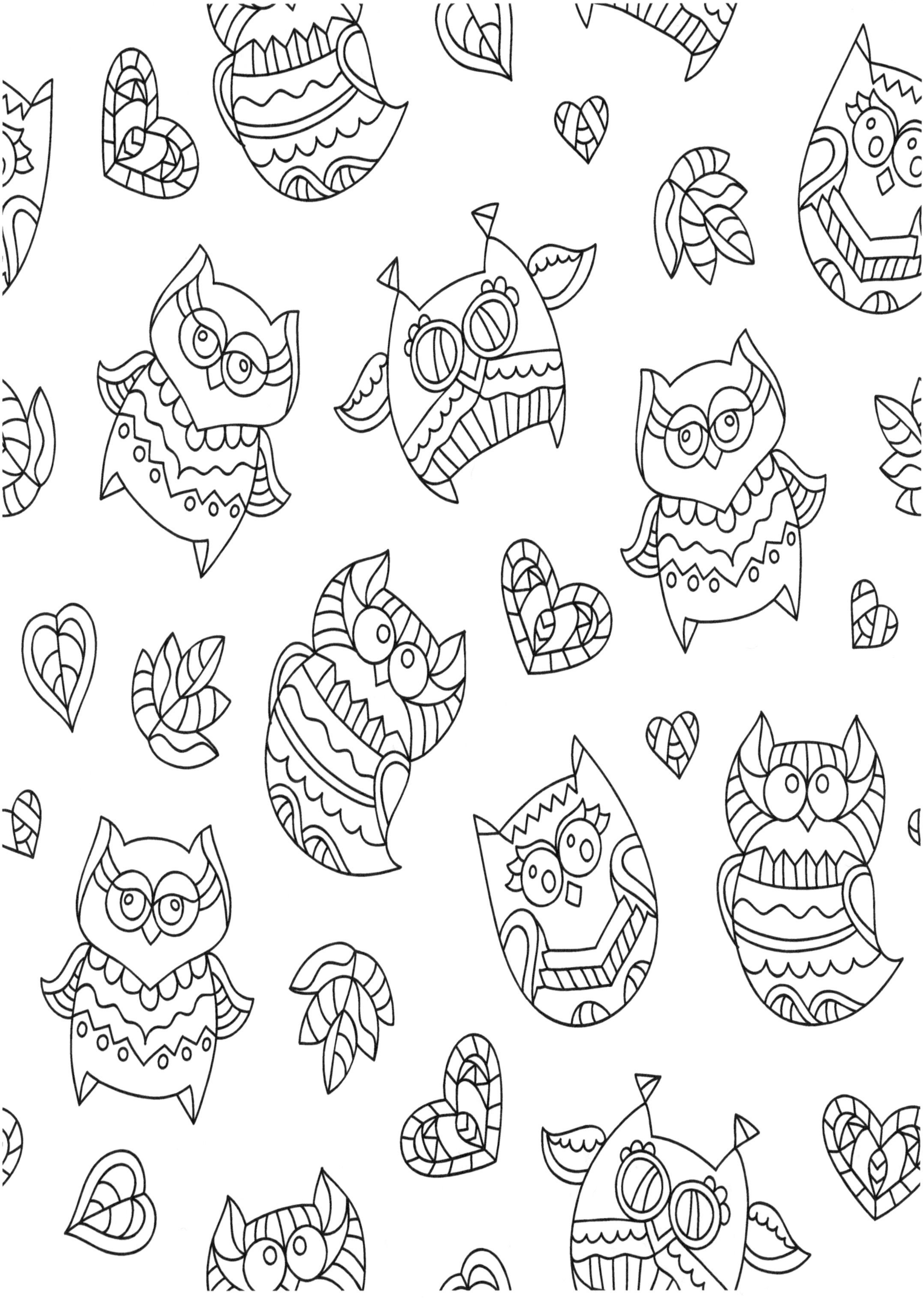

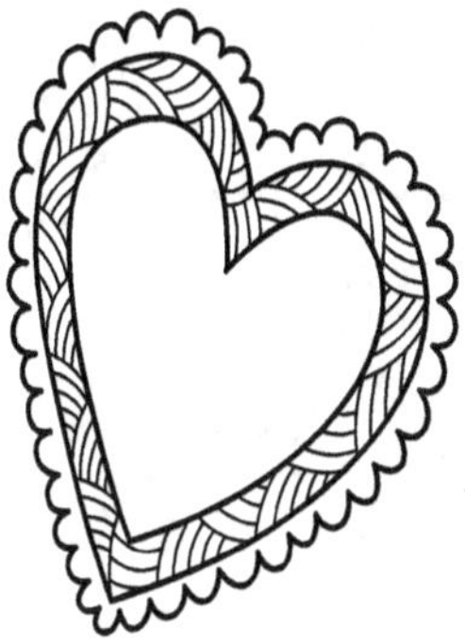

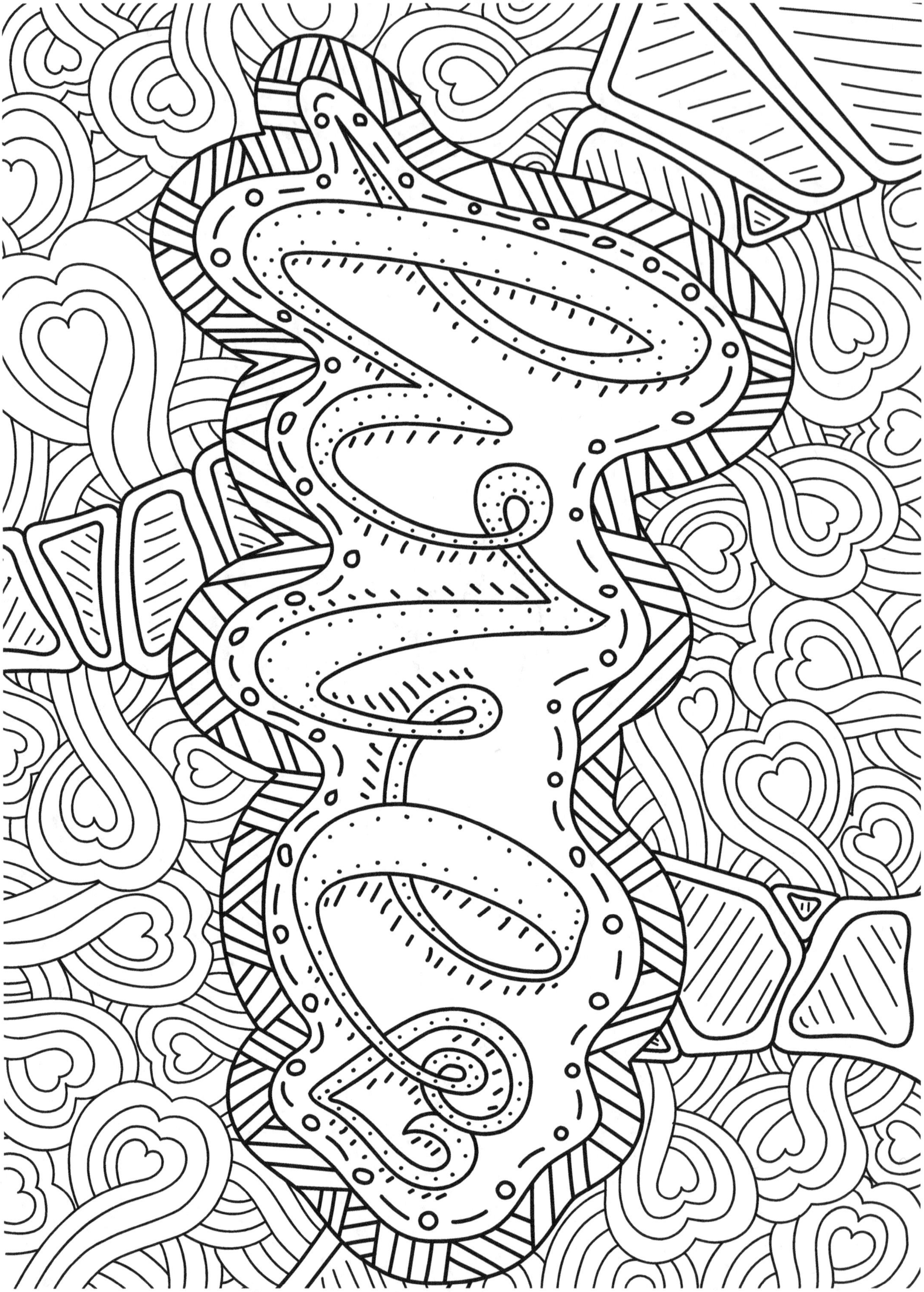
love

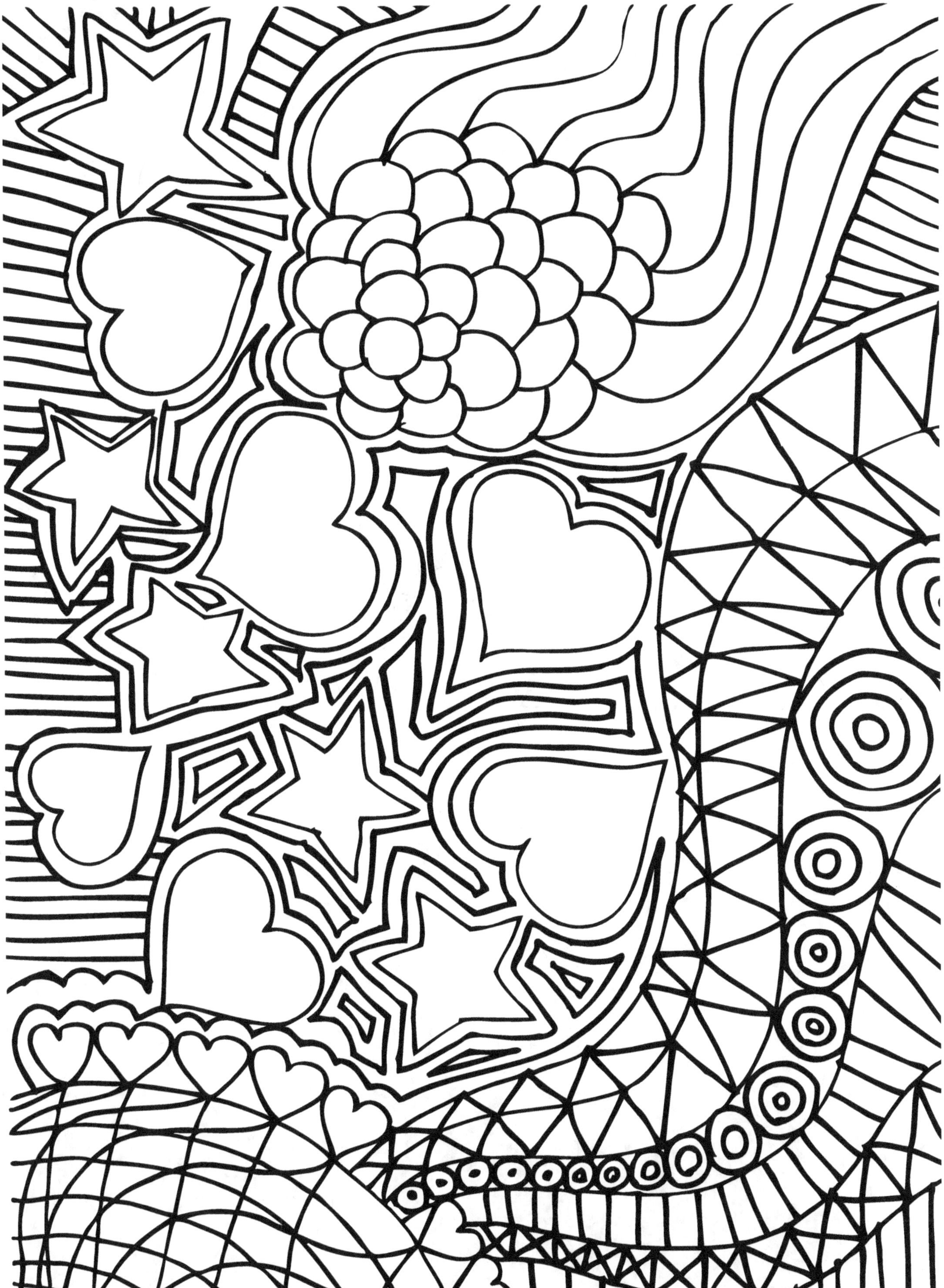

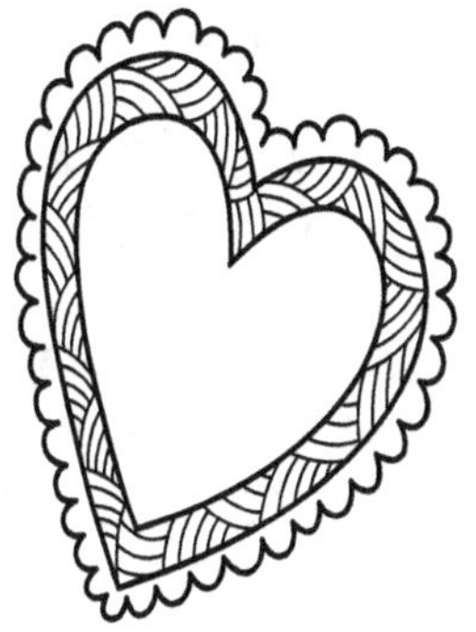

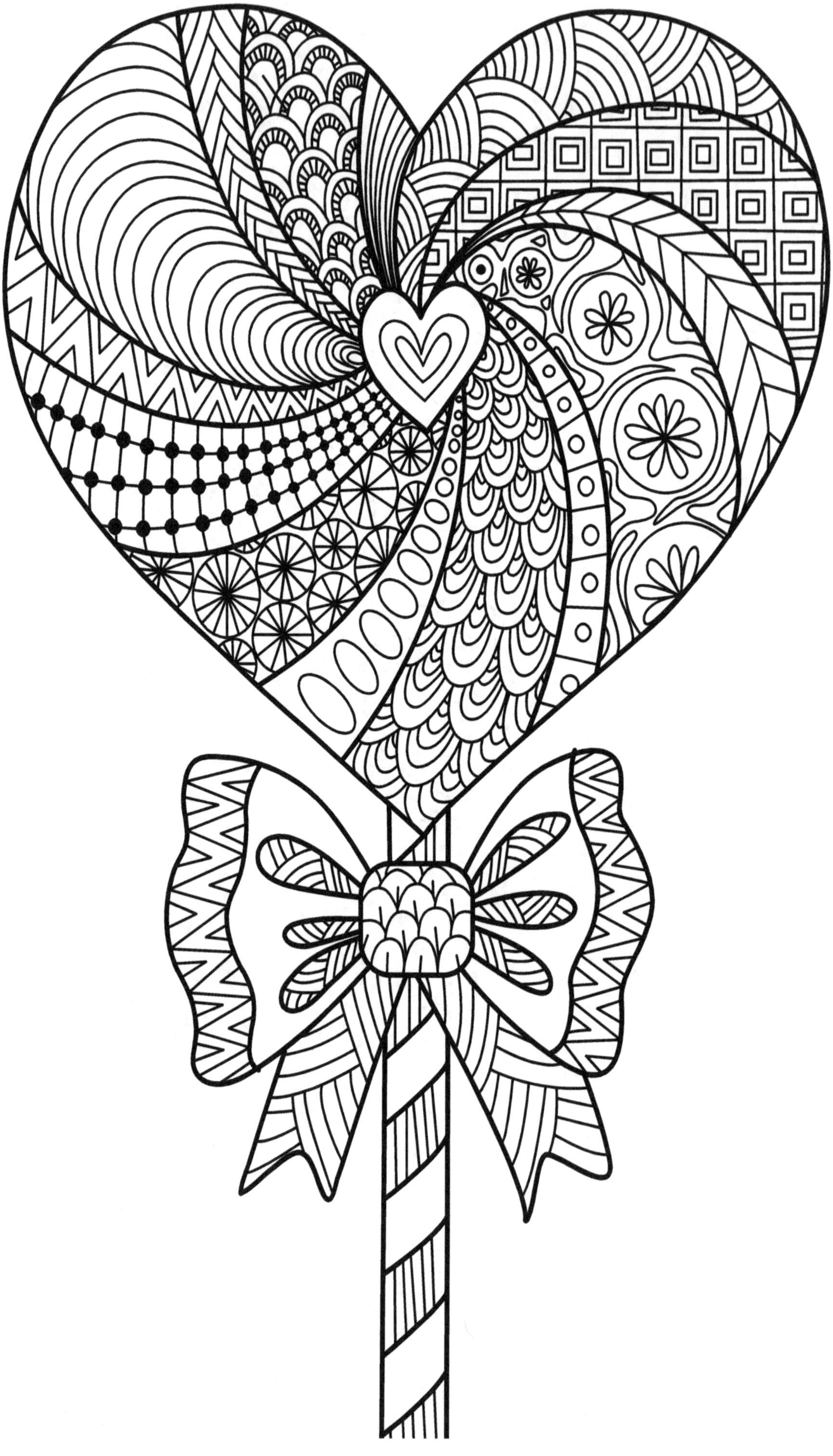

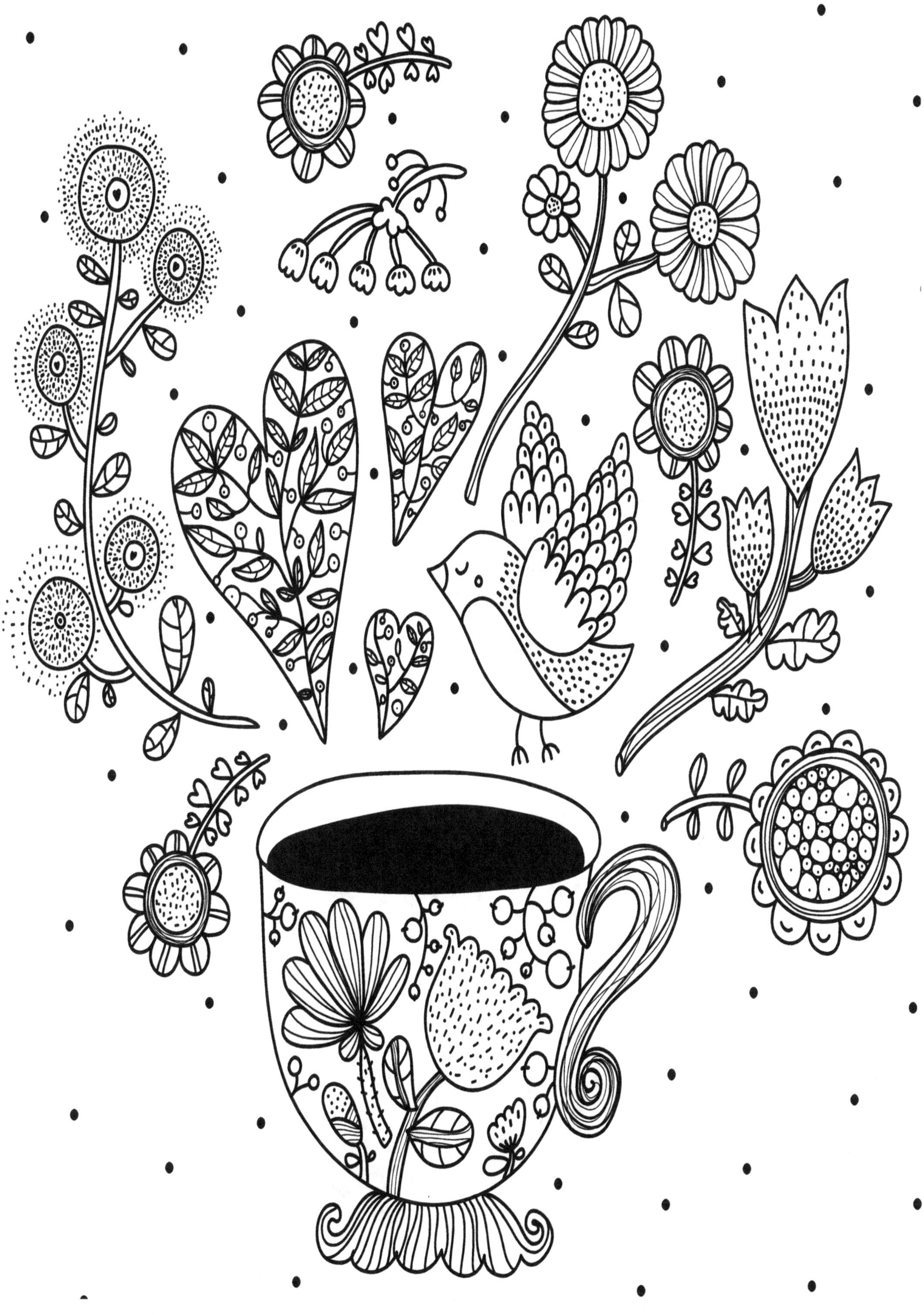

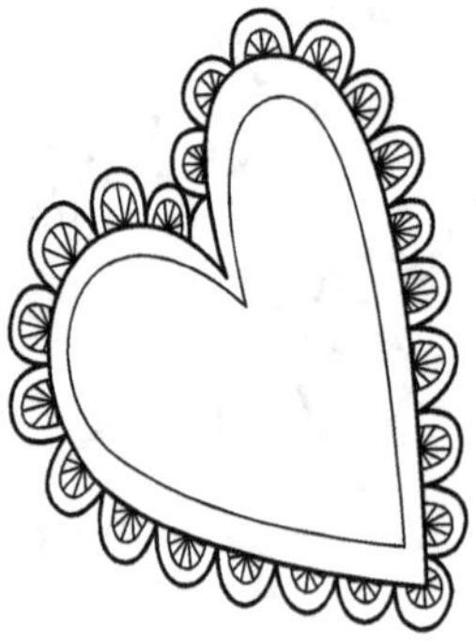

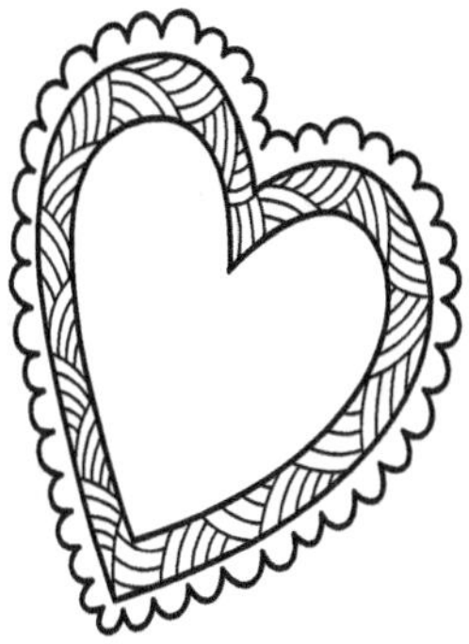

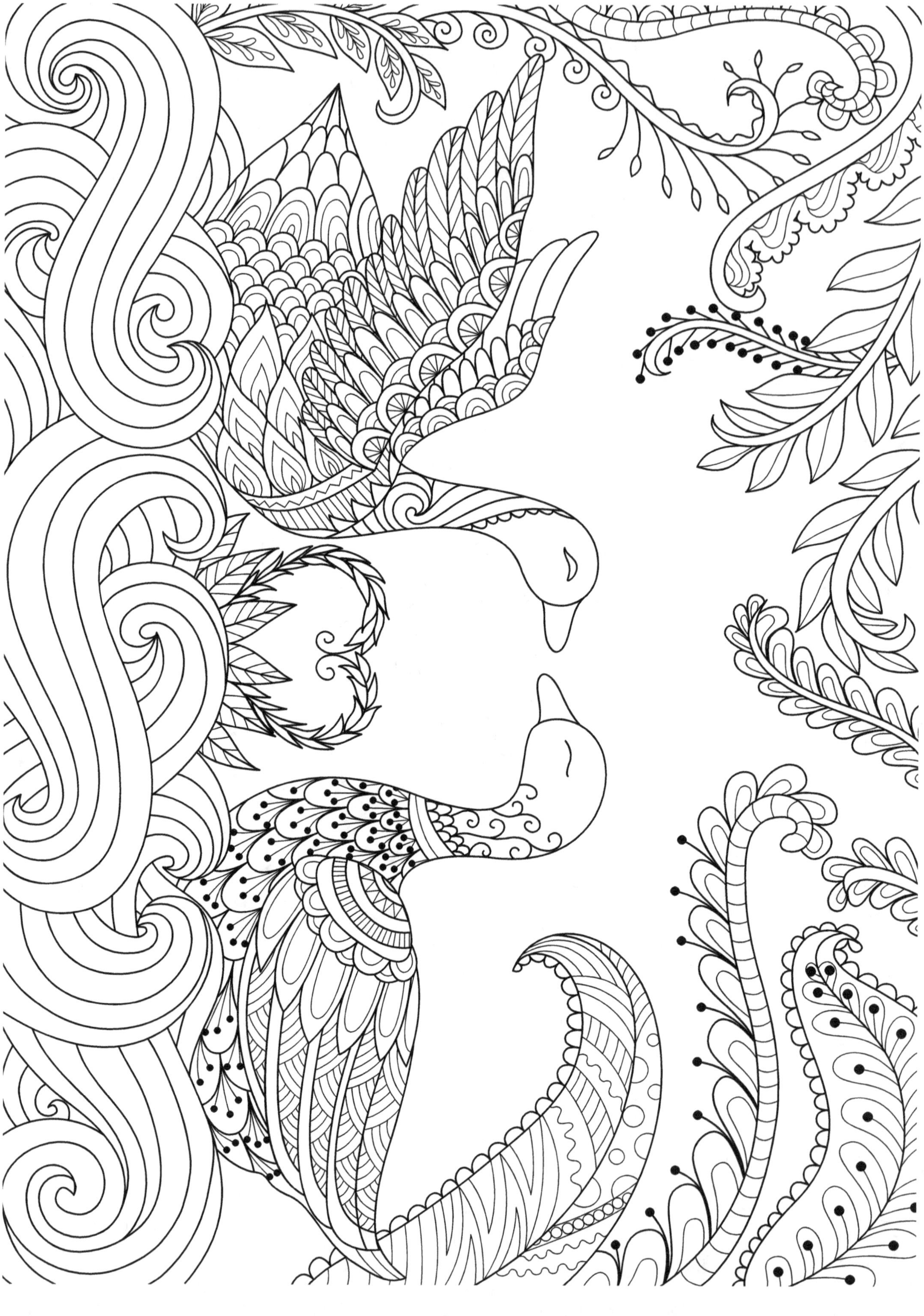

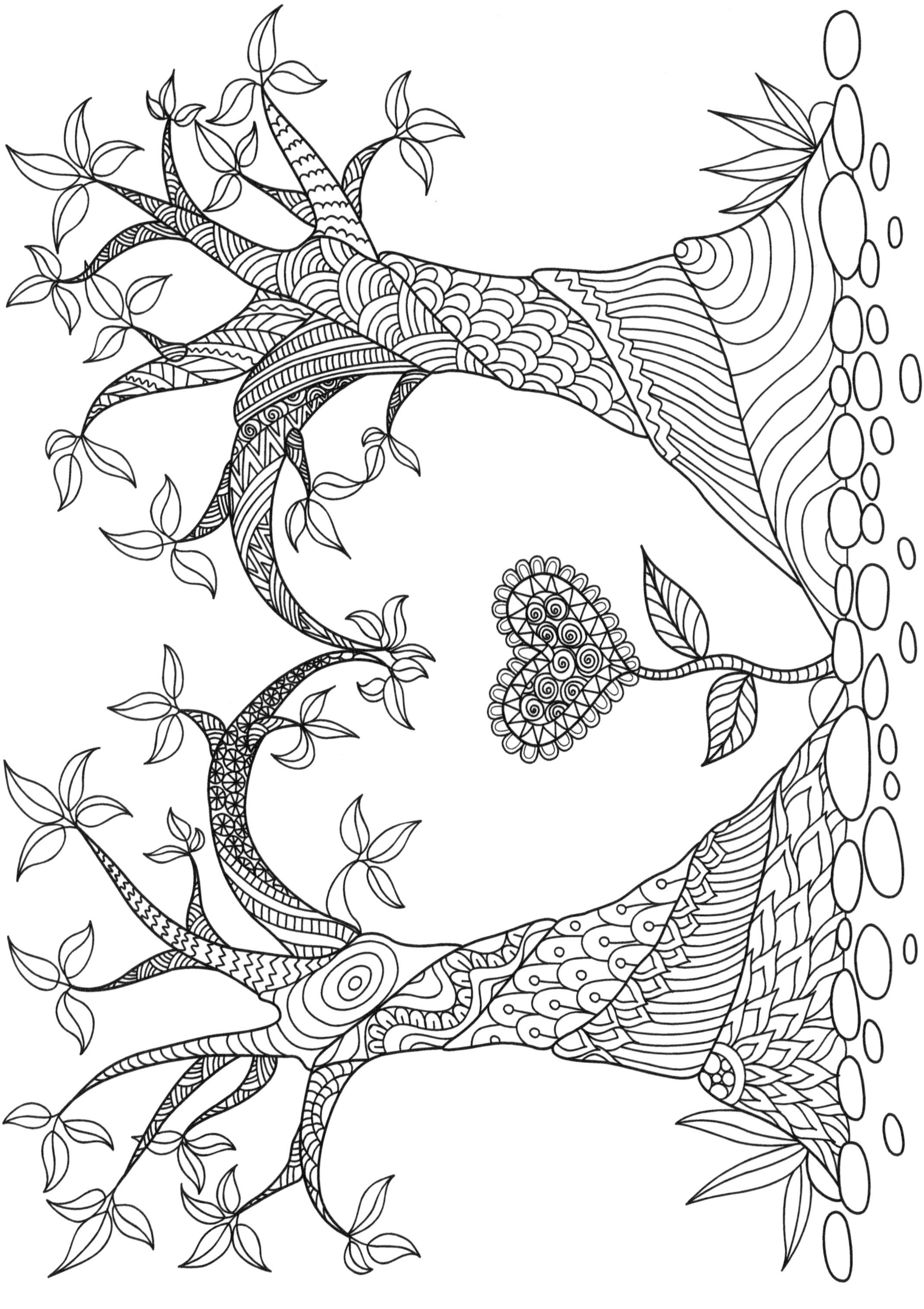

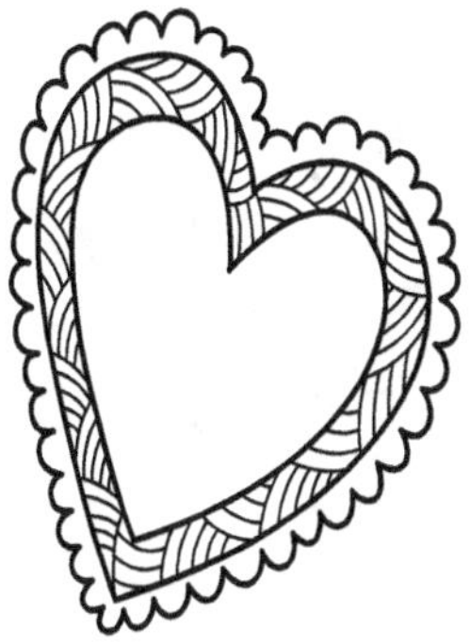

VE
Fly
Dream

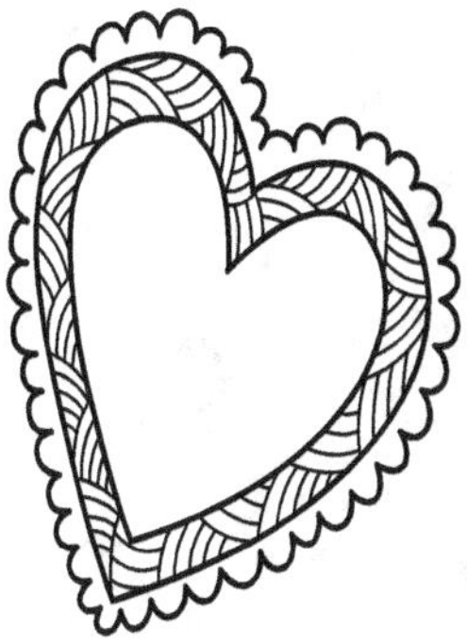

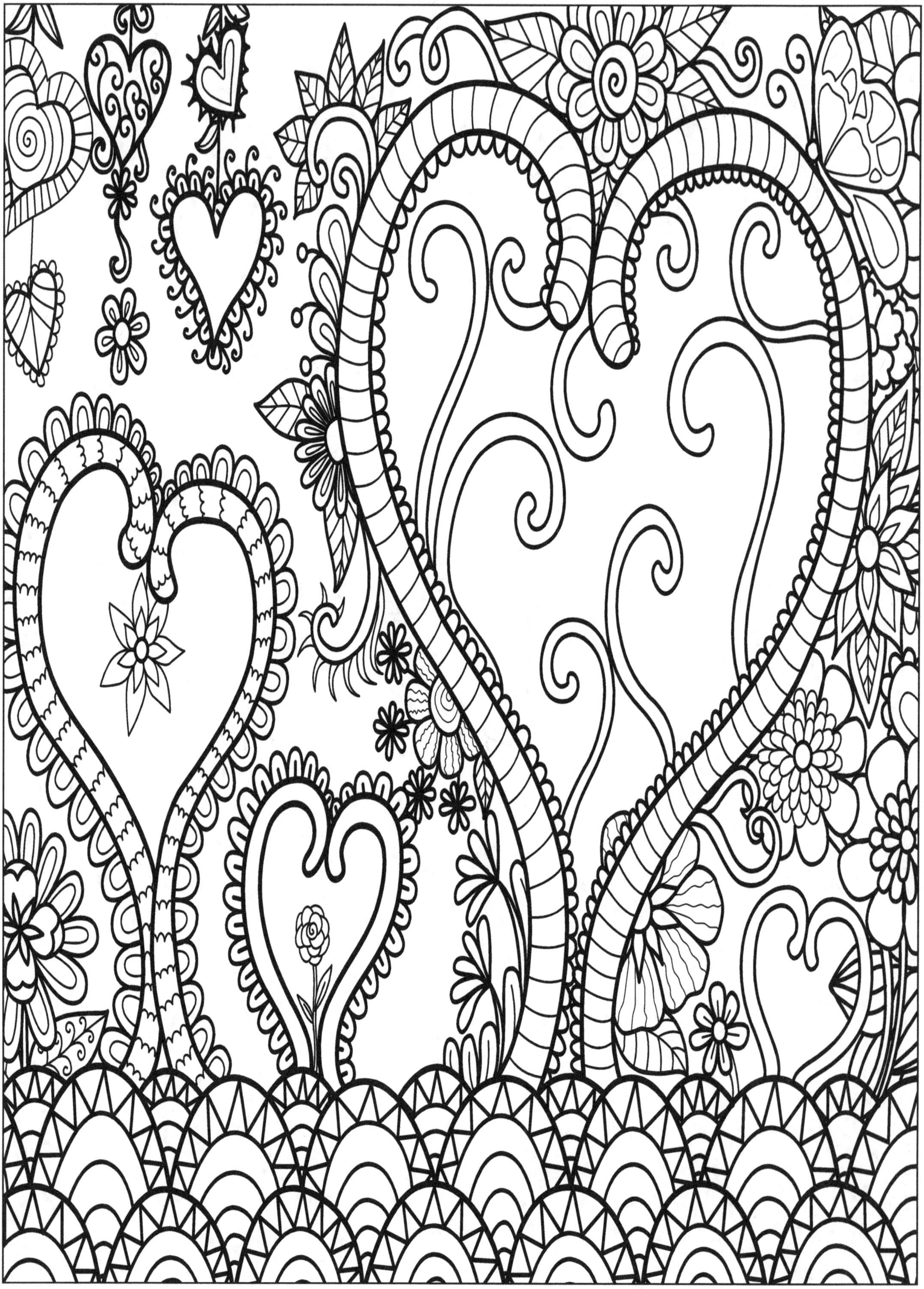

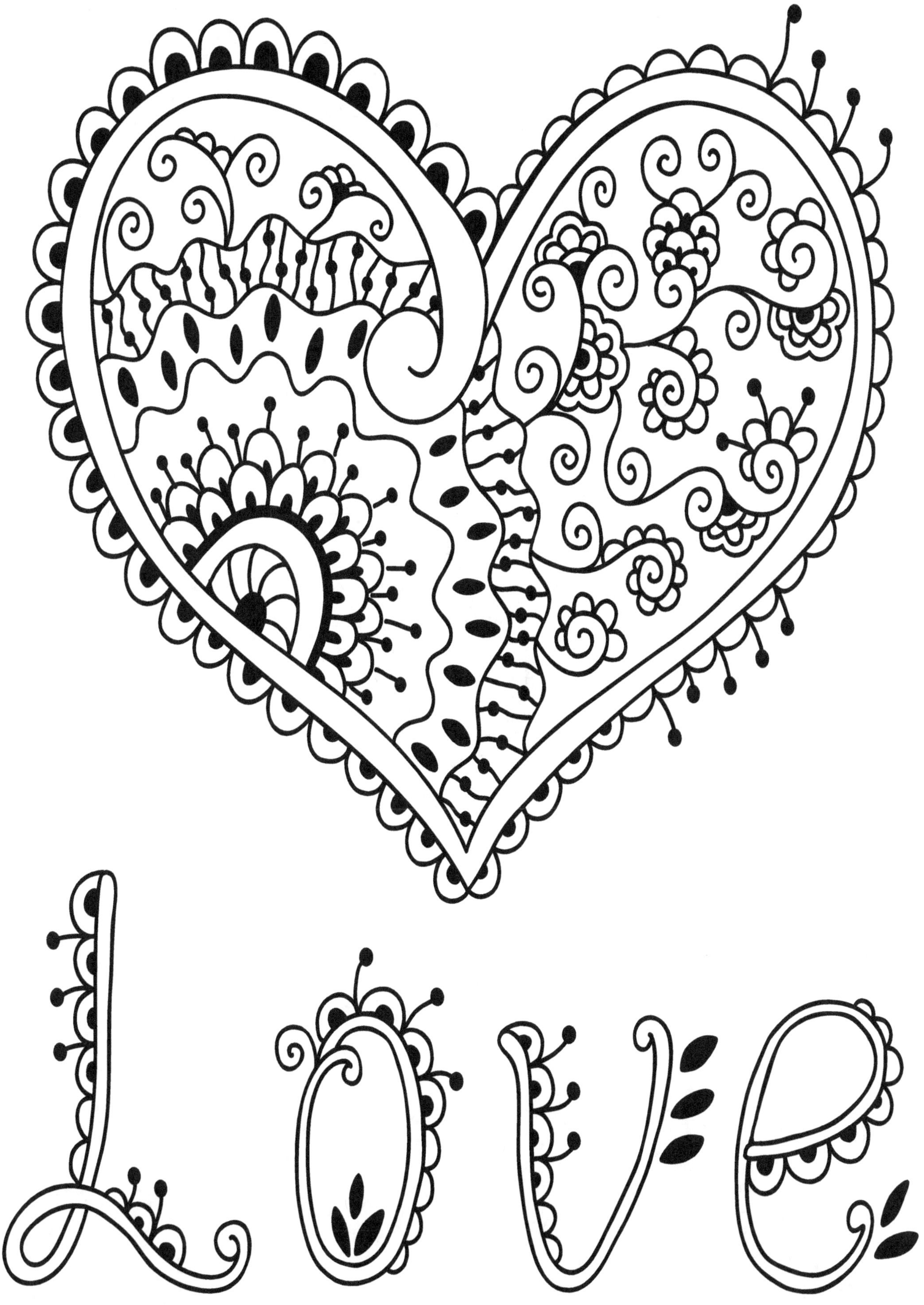
Love

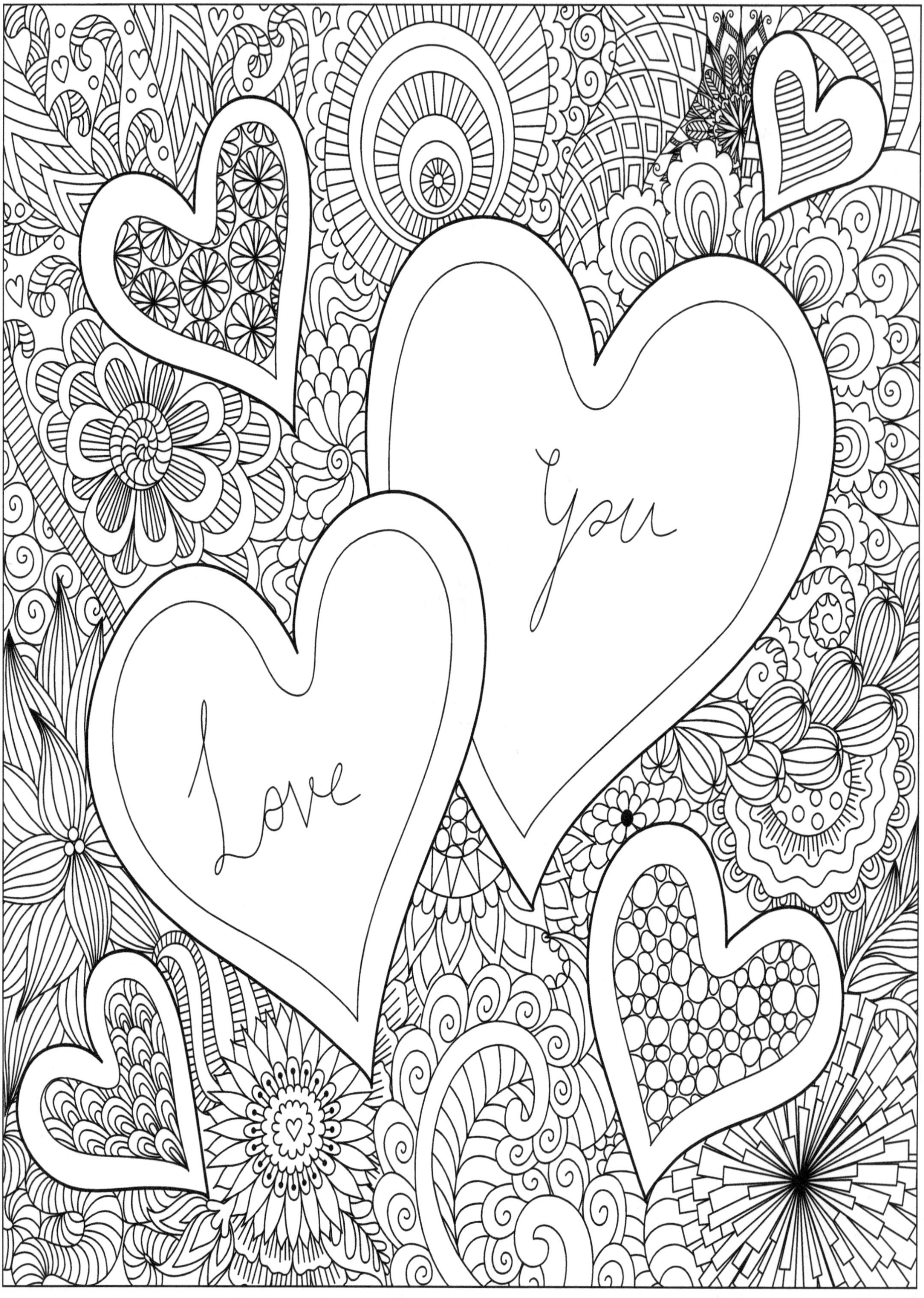
You
Love

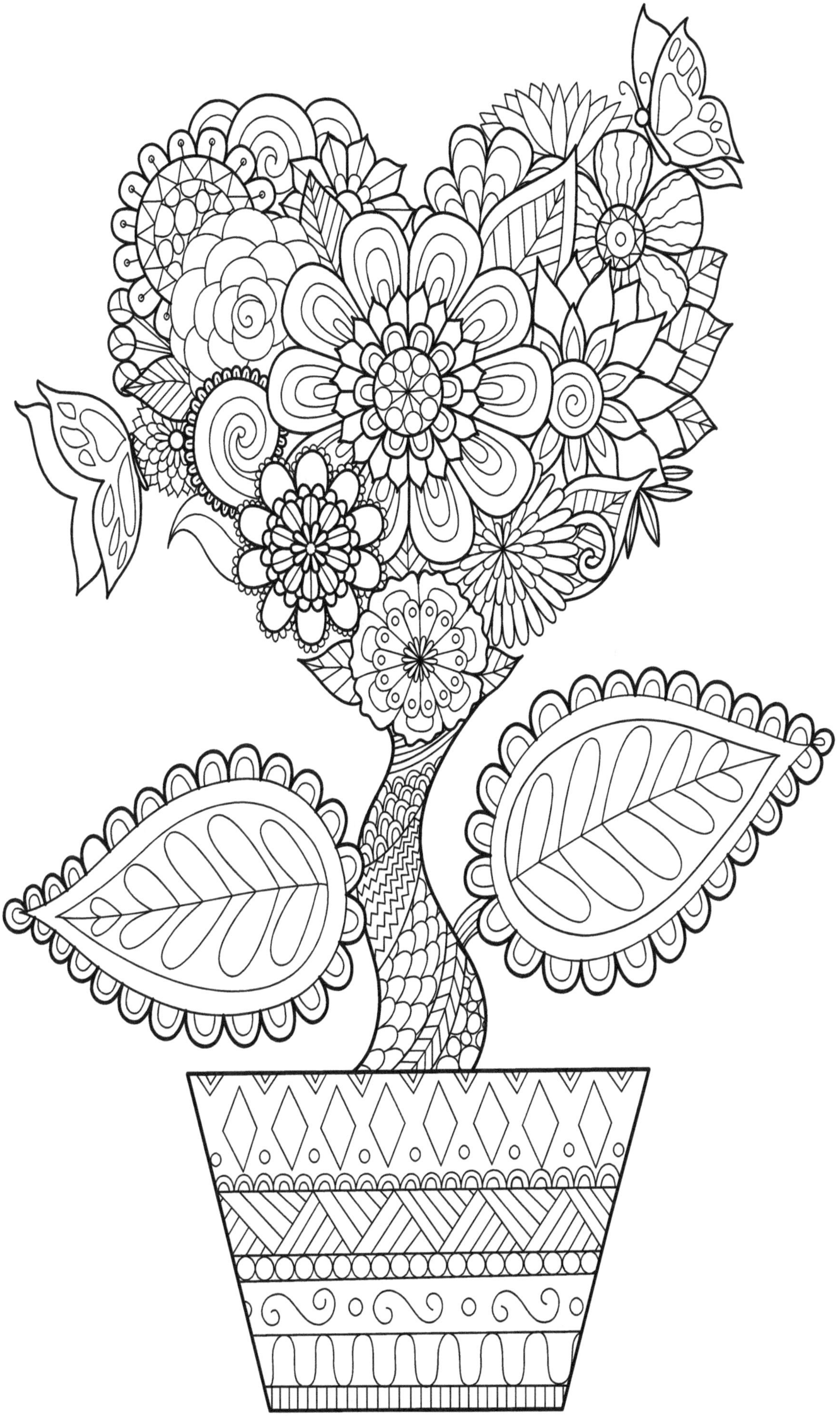

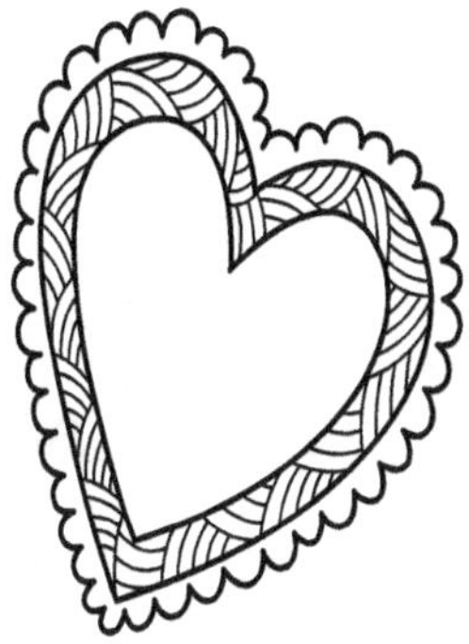

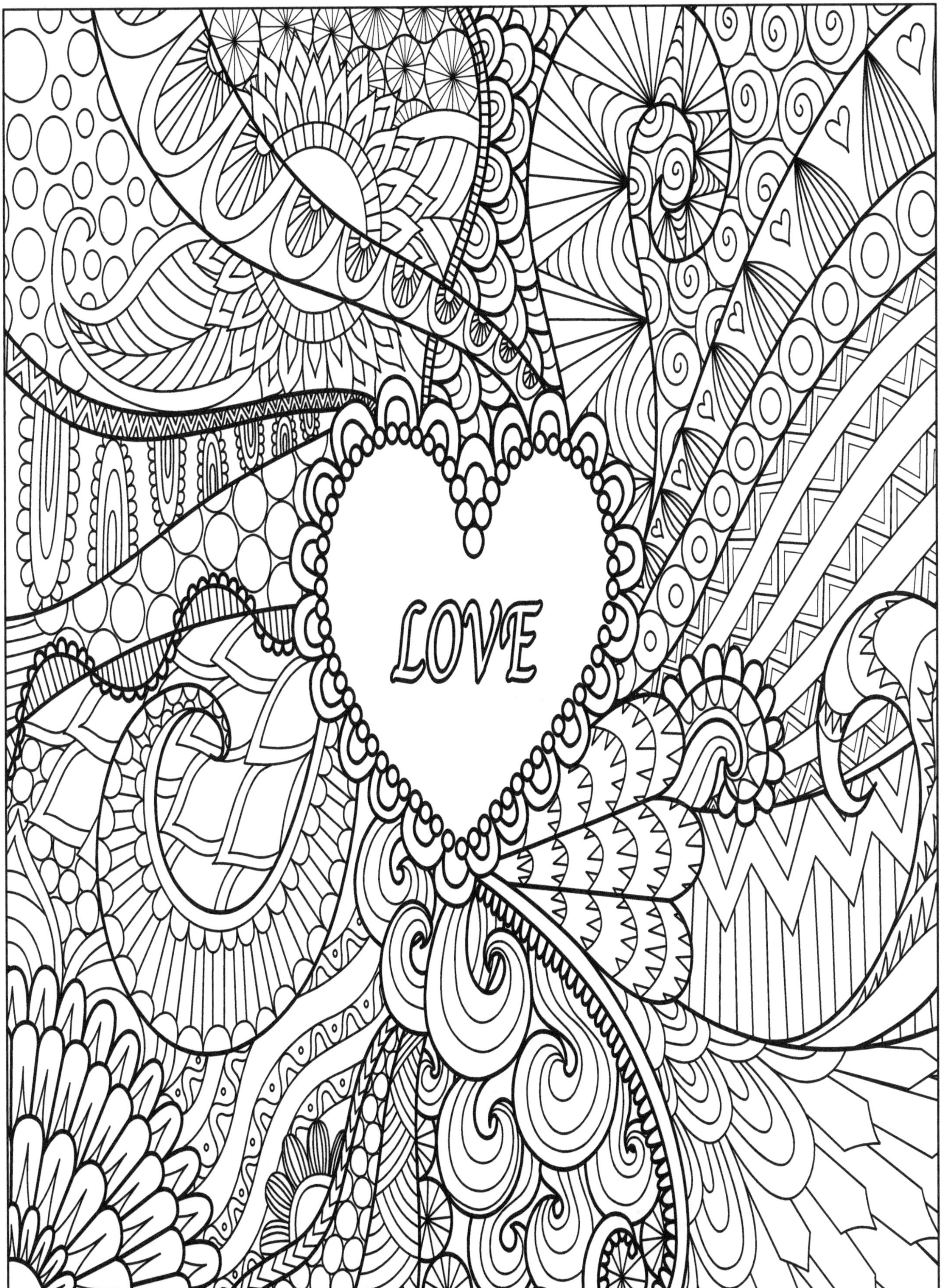
LOVE

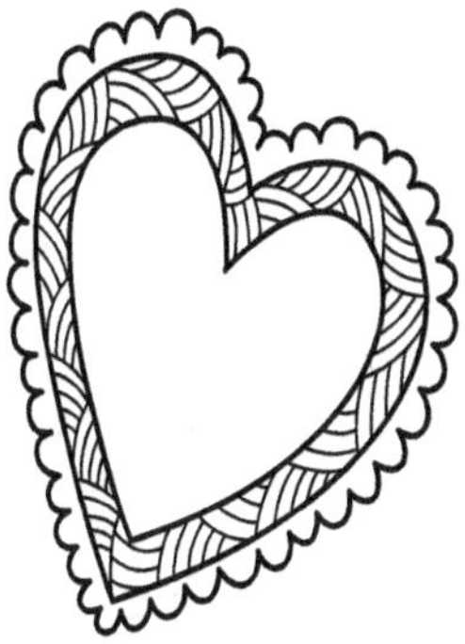

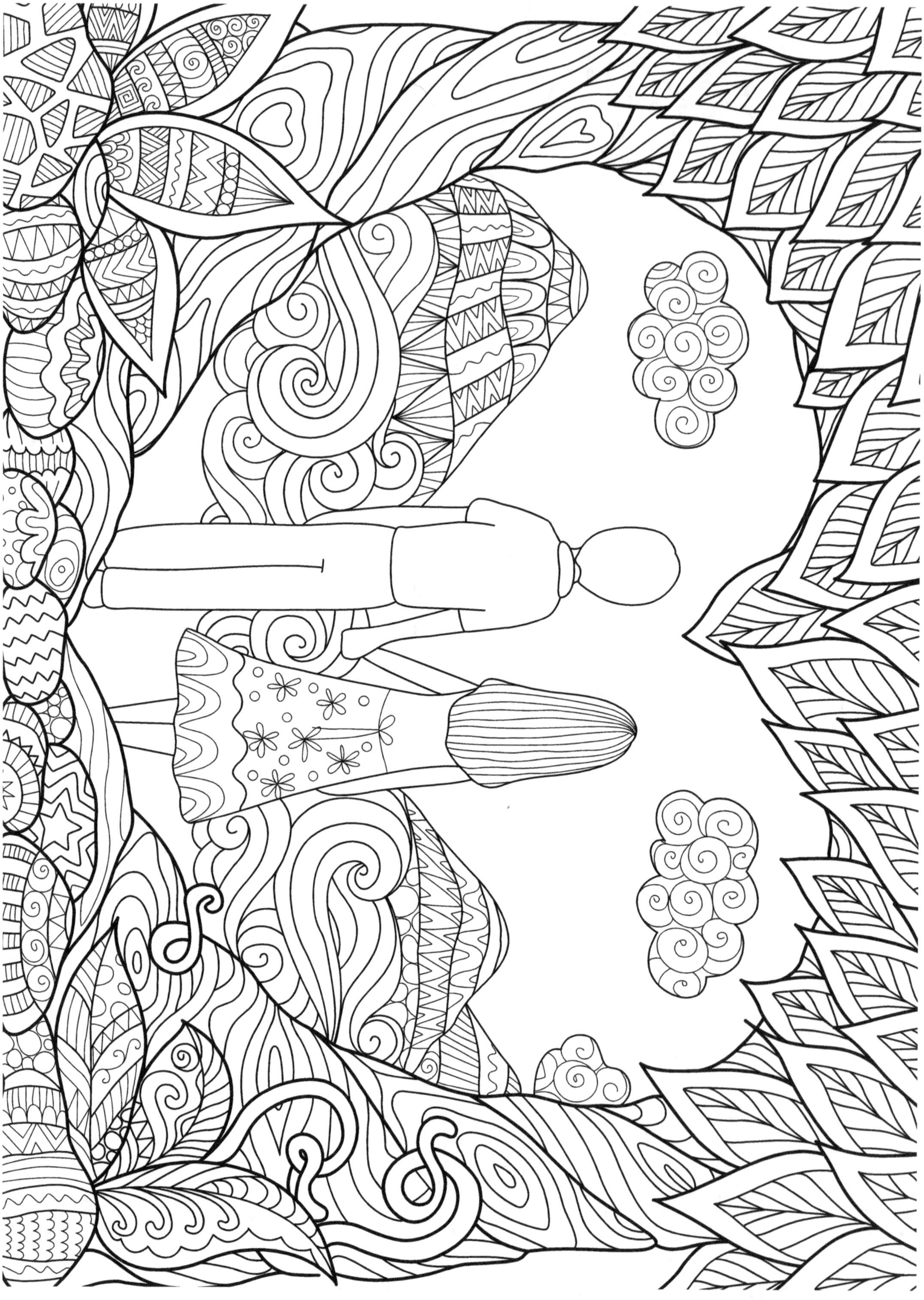

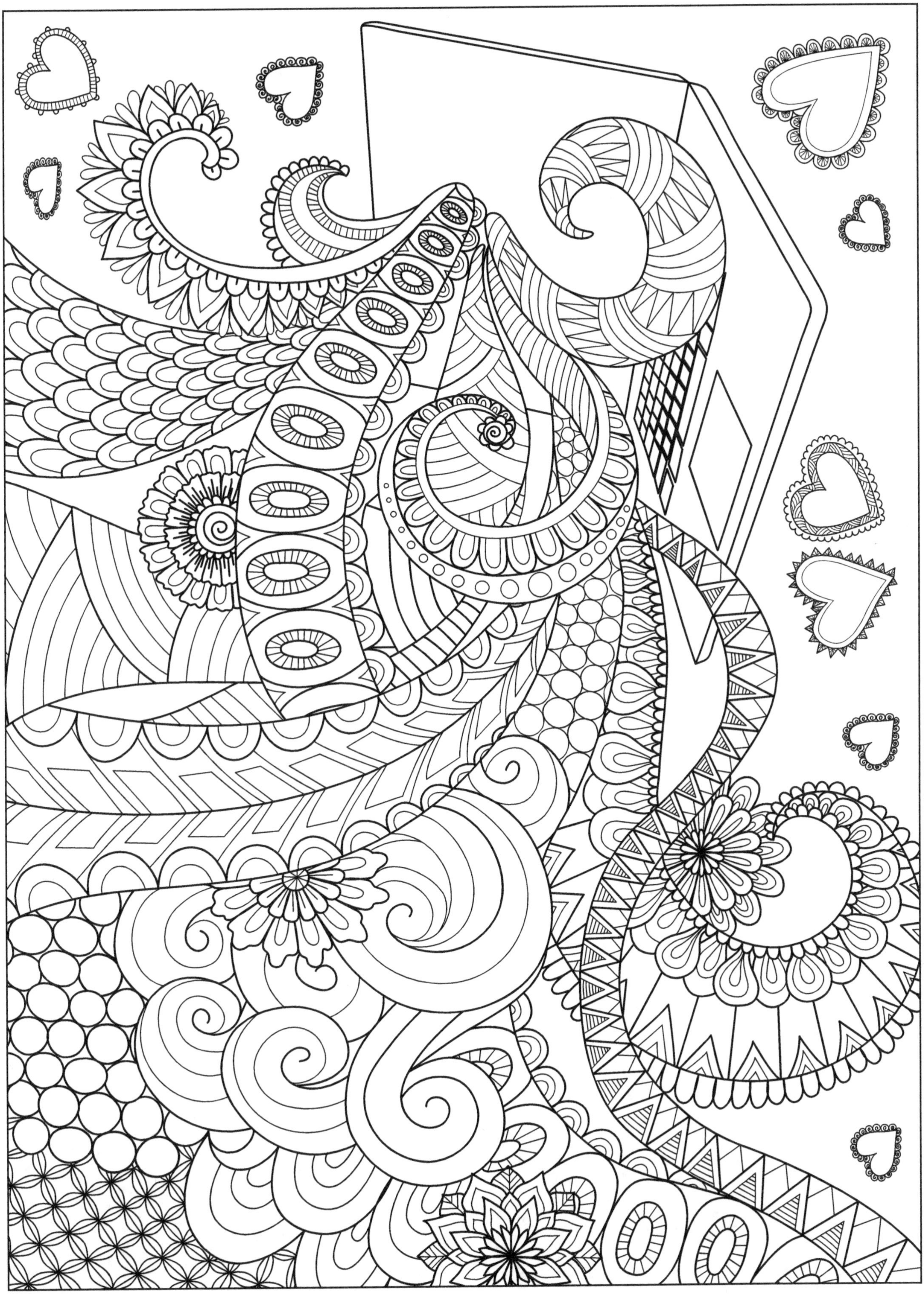

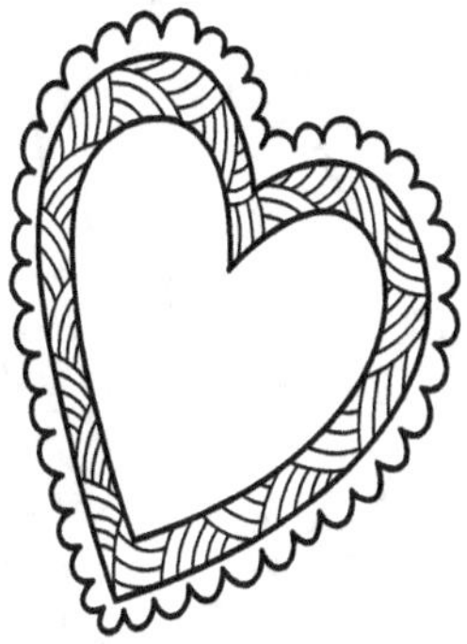

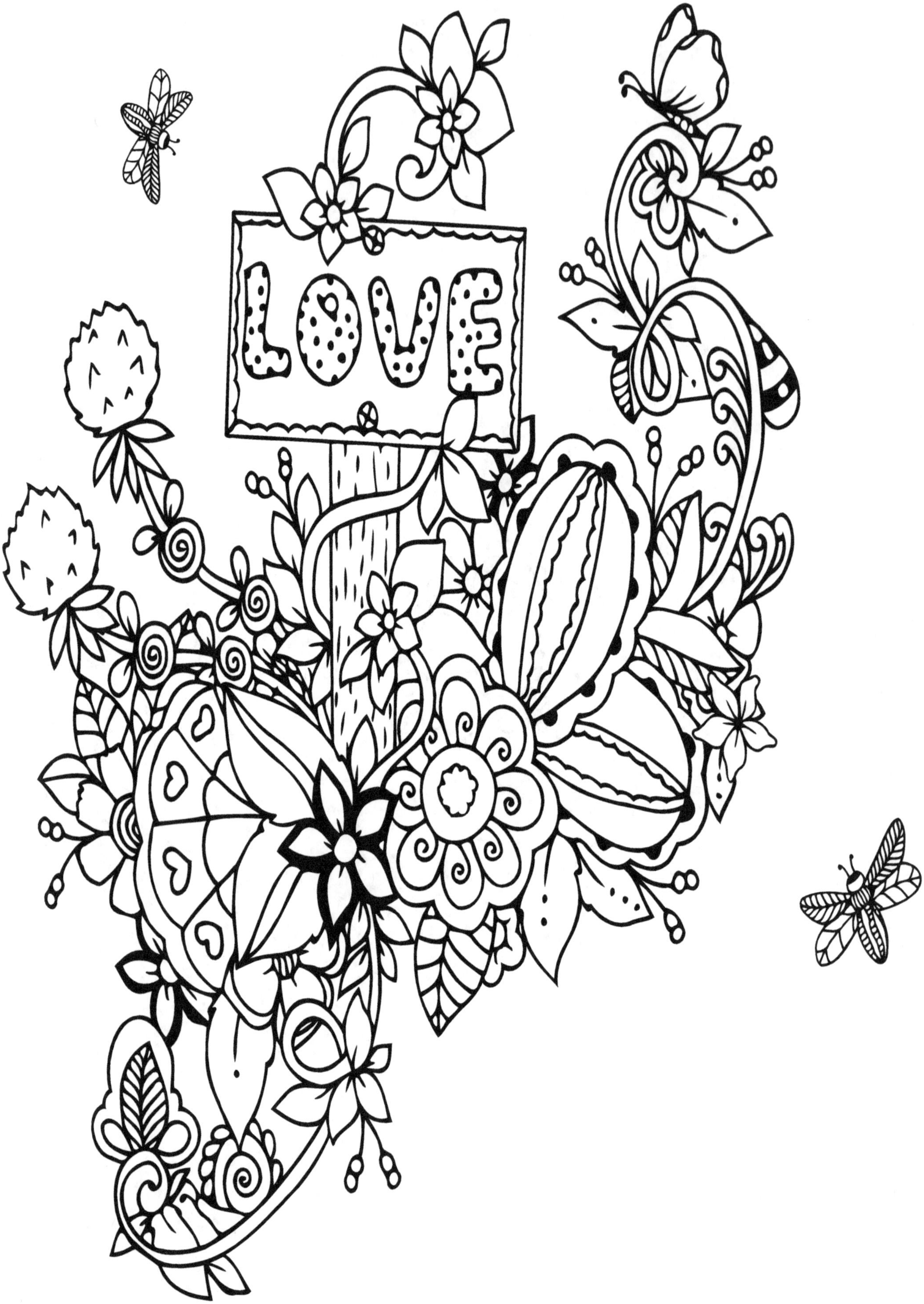
LOVE

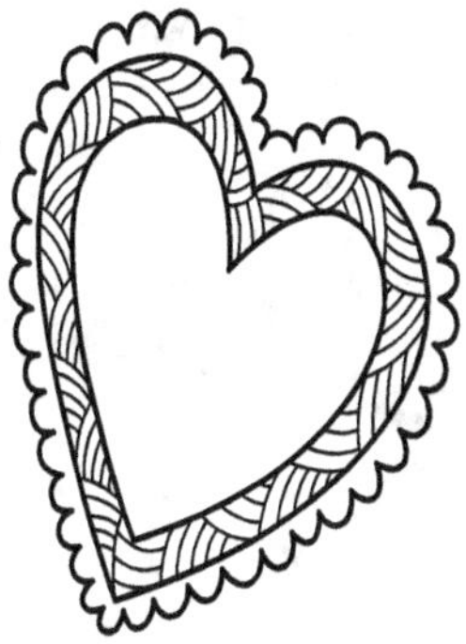

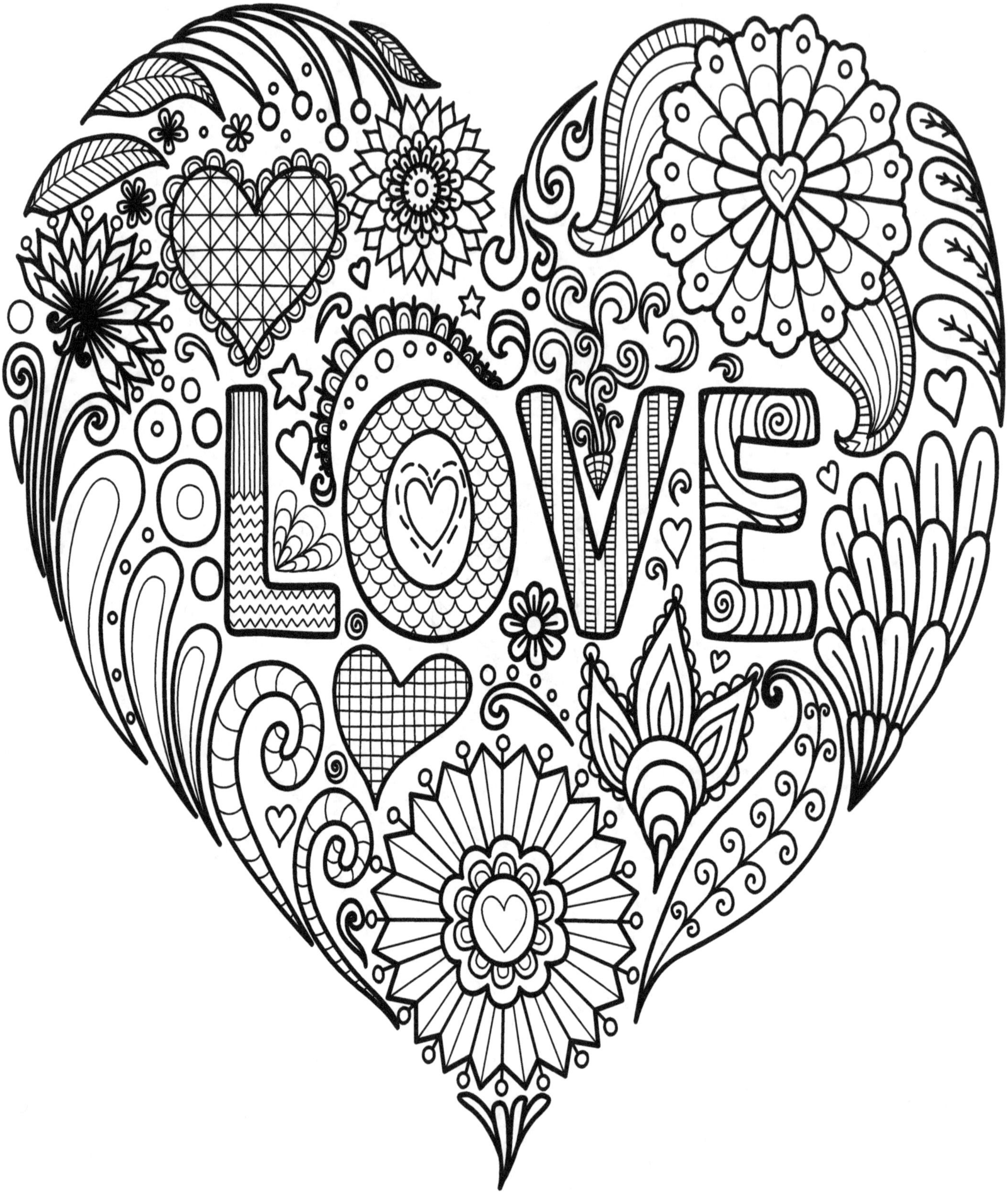
LOVE

LOVE IS IN THE AIR!

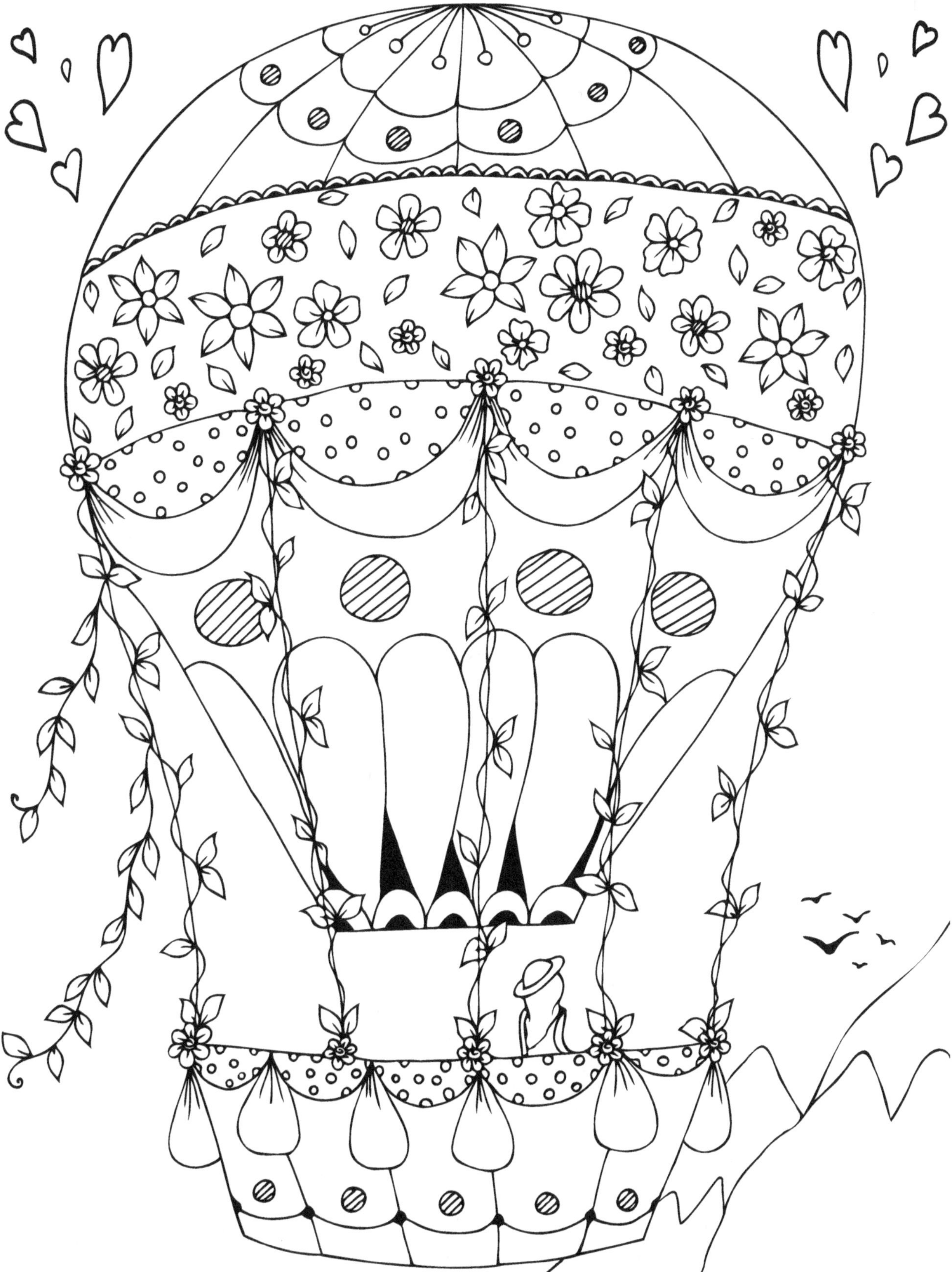

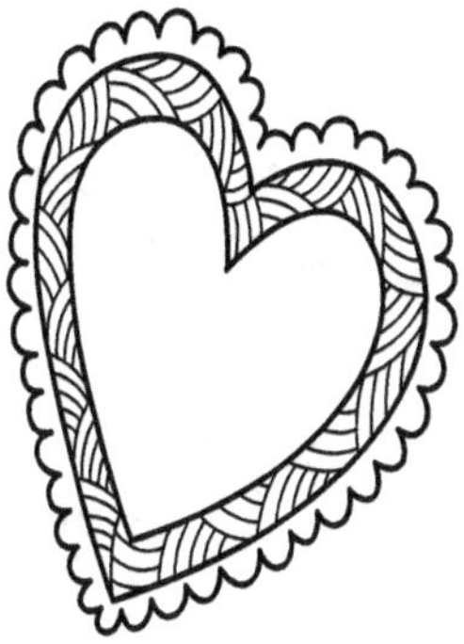

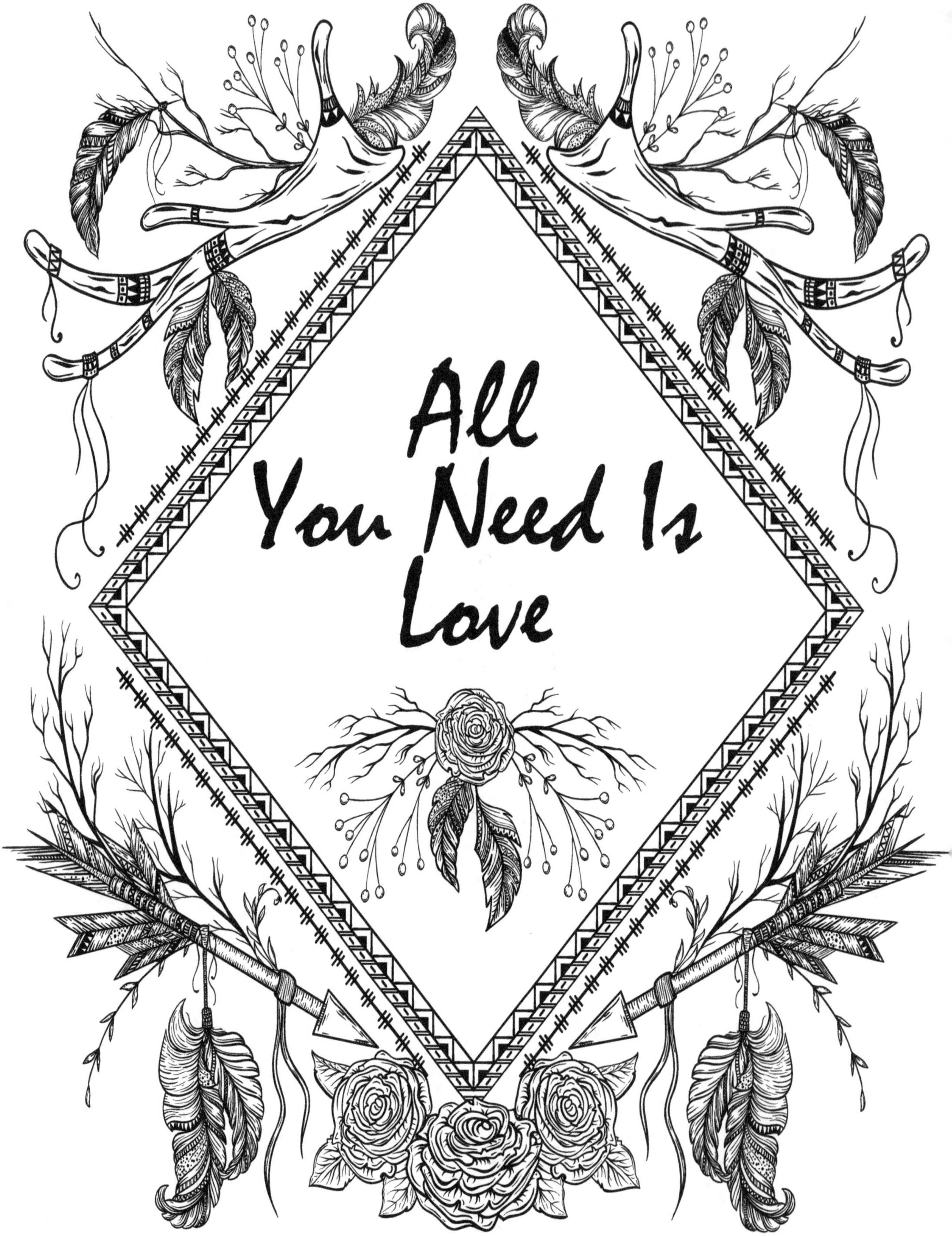

adventurelearningpress.com